THE *Continuous* ATONEMENT

THE *Continuous* ATONEMENT

Christ doesn't just make *up* the difference.
He makes *all* the difference.

BRAD WILCOX

DESERET
BOOK
SALT LAKE CITY, UTAH

Visit us at DeseretBook.com

Library of Congress Cataloging-in-Publication Data

Wilcox, Brad.
The continuous atonement / Brad Wilcox.
p. cm.
Includes bibliographical references and index.
ISBN 978-1-60641-037-0 (hardbound : alk. paper)
1. Atonement—Church of Jesus Christ of Latter-day Saints.
2. Repentance—Church of Jesus Christ of Latter-day Saints. I. Title.
BX8643.A85W55 2009
232'.3—dc22

2008046940

Printed in the United States of America
R. R. Donnelley and Sons, Crawfordsville, IN

30

To Wendee
who once spoke along with me on this topic
at BYU Women's Conference
and
To Scott
who once needed to remember the
"hope smiling brightly before us"

CONTENTS

ACKNOWLEDGMENTS

First, I acknowledge you for choosing to read this book. As a mission president, I always found it interesting that after I had reminded the missionaries of a rule or standard, it was the ones *without* the problem who would feel guilty, apologize, and commit to do better. The ones for whom the reminder was intended usually remained oblivious to the need for change.

I've been told the gospel is here to comfort the afflicted and afflict the comfortable. I can think of times in my life when I have found great comfort in the words of the Savior and His prophets. I can also think of times when, like the oblivious missionaries, I've needed a little afflicting. One can always locate plenty of scriptures and sermons for both occasions.

Elder Dallin H. Oaks has written: "A call for repentance that is clear enough and loud enough to encourage reformation by the lenient can produce paralyzing discouragement in the conscientious. The dose of doctrine that is strong enough to penetrate the hard shell of the easygoing group may prove to be a massive overdose for the conscientious" (*With Full Purpose of Heart*, 129).

Perhaps some could misconstrue the hopeful message of this book as a reason to postpone making needed changes, but my greater fear is that those who are honestly trying to improve will become discouraged if no one communicates hope loudly and clearly. I seriously doubt that many of the "lenient" and "easygoing" would take time to read a book like this. They are probably a bit too busy eating, drinking, and being merry to want to be reminded about the Savior. I choose to assume those reading these words are the soft-shelled survivors of many a massive doctrinal overdose focusing on the "Thou shalts" and the "Thou shalt nots." Let's leave the afflicting for another day. The purpose of this book is to comfort.

It is said that authors don't choose their topics, their topics choose them. Certainly that was the case for the topics included in this book, which have filled my mind during every spare moment for many years. The concepts expressed here have often been the focus of my personal study, prayers, and celestial room conversations. Rough drafts have been written on scraps of paper, in margins of books, and in my mind while driving long distances. And that's where they would have stayed were it not for the help of many dear friends.

Heartfelt thanks to four friends in particular whose encouragement kept me going: Nancy Bayles, who heard me speak about some of these ideas and said, "You need to write a book"; Brett Sanders, who also listened early on and said, "This needs to be a book"; Emily Watts, who believed in me when I proposed my first outline; and Robert L. Millet, who reviewed my rough drafts and said, "Brad, this needs to be a book."

My family members are always my first editors. Thanks to my supportive wife, Debi, and our children: Wendee and Gian, Russell and Trish, Whitney, and David, as well as Val C. Wilcox and Leroy and Mary Lois Gunnell. Robert and Helen Wells, Sharla Nuttall, Kellie Harman, Lorna Stock, Carson Twitchell, Nate Sanders, and Steven Edwards also made significant contributions. Special thanks to my friends Sharon Black, who pushed me to clarify content as well as mechanics; Eula Ewing Monroe, whose perspective was invaluable; and Bobbi Redick, whose help on this manuscript was truly a labor of love.

It is a joy to serve in the stake presidency of the BYU 4th Stake along with Tracy T. Ward, Barnard N. Madsen, William W. Bridges, Boyd J. Holdaway, and Jeffrey G. Jones. I appreciate the dedication of these wonderful men and the outstanding young people we serve.

Finally, thanks to prophets, leaders, teachers, and artists who have spoken and written so beautifully about the Atonement. Each explanation, example, and presentation helped me understand more and draw closer to Heavenly Father and Jesus. The preparation of this manuscript has changed the way I pray, ponder, partake of the sacrament, and speak about the Savior—all evidence of how the Atonement is slowly but surely changing me.

INTRODUCTION

"I'll never do it again," we say—and then we do it. "Now I really mean it. I'll never do it again," and then we do it. "This has got to stop. I swear I will never do it again." And we do it. When we or those we love are stuck in cycles of compulsive behavior, it is easy to become discouraged and feel like giving up. We fast, pray, seek blessings, and still wonder if the needed changes will ever occur. When they finally do, we wonder if the positive changes will last. At low points we want to quit—or worse, we just stop caring altogether. Those are the moments when we need to remember there is always hope. As President Dieter F. Uchtdorf declared, "No matter how bleak the chapter of our lives may look today, because of the life and sacrifice of Jesus Christ, we may hope and be assured that the ending of the book of our lives will exceed our grandest expectations" ("Infinite Power of Hope," 22–23).

We don't have to pretend there is no God, or desperately try to find reasons why the Church is not true in order to avoid change. We don't have to seek out others who are struggling so we feel justified, or hate those who aren't struggling so we can feel better. We don't have to surrender to addiction and hate ourselves, as easy as that is to do. Instead, we have to let faith be an anchor for our souls (see Ether 12:4).

Changes in belief always precede changes in behavior. Steadfastness and good works come from hope, and hope flows from faith—but not just any faith. Many people believe in God. They even like to share stories about God and angels over the Internet. Still, for so many, their professed faith doesn't affect or change them. It rarely alters their choices. They believe in a higher power, but without knowing Him, they are limited in accessing that higher power.

Joseph Smith taught that *true* faith is more than knowing there is a God. It is knowing God—knowing His attributes and His relationship to us. It is knowing that He has a plan for us and that we are living in accordance with that plan (see *Lectures on Faith*, 3:2–5).

Students of the Bible read, "Be still, and know that I am God" (Psalm 46:10). Joseph Smith taught that the reverse is also true: Know God, and then be still. When we come to know God, His prophets, plan, and eternal purposes for us, then we can indeed be still.

It is one thing to *follow* Christ and another thing entirely to be *led* by Him. Latter-day Saints are led by Christ in the same way He has always led His people—through living prophets and apostles. That authoritative leadership sets our faith apart.

Just as Joseph Smith defined a true faith in God, I testify that a true faith in Christ is more than just knowing about Him or even believing He is divine. It is knowing that His Atonement is real, that its purpose is to transform us, and that it will be available as long as that perfecting process takes. We have a Savior who covers us, a Redeemer who changes us, and a Good Shepherd who is willing to go in search of us again and again—continuously.

Gethsemane, Calvary, the empty tomb—we cannot seriously reflect on the sacred and monumental events that occurred in these special locations without feeling a deep and overwhelming sense of gratitude and humility. With great reverence we read of *what* happened, but try as we might, we cannot begin to approach an understanding of *how* it happened. In this respect, the Atonement is incomprehensible. However, its effects in our lives need not be. We can and must understand how the Atonement acts as a constant force for good. We must recognize it as a gift from a loving Savior who will never give up on us. As my friend Kenneth Cope has written:

Tell me, tell of a God that won't slow down,
That will not rest till I am found.
Tell of His heart that won't let go,
His arms that long to hold me.
("Tell Me")

Truly, our Heavenly Father and Jesus Christ will not rest until we are found. So if at first you don't succeed—if at second, third, or fourth you don't succeed either, don't find excuses. Find the Savior and the blessings of His continuous Atonement.

Chapter 1

HOWEVER LONG IT TAKES

Perfection is our long-term goal, but for now our goal is progress in that direction—continuous progress that is possible only through the continuous Atonement.

The sixteen-year-old looked nice in his new suit purchased for this special occasion—his first time blessing the sacrament. The young priest tried to look calm, but his Adam's apple bobbed up and down as often as his eyes blinked.

The organist played the introduction to the hymn, and the chorister led the congregation in singing. Four priests stood at the sacrament table and carefully folded back the lace cloth to reveal trays containing the bread. Silently, the young men began to break the bread, with the new priest looking nervously from his own hands to the hands of the experienced boys, who were moving more quickly.

When the hymn ended, the organist played a reverent interlude in order to give the new priest time to finish. The others were finished with the bread in their trays and had even completed a few additional ones. The boy felt the eyes of the whole congregation on him as he tried to hurry.

Finally he dropped to his knees to read the prayer. "O God, the Eternal Father," he began. His voice sounded shaky and unsure. "We ask thee in the name of Jesus Christ—" Silence. Although few members of the congregation could recite the sacrament prayers from memory, most were familiar enough with them that they could recognize when something didn't sound quite right. So could the young priest. So could his companions. So could the bishop—to whom the boy now looked for direction.

The bishop made eye contact and nodded gently, indicating that the young man should begin again. He did. "O God, the Eternal Father, we ask thee in the name of thy Son, Jesus Christ, to bless and sanctify this water—" Silence. He was blessing the bread. By now even the children in the congregation were feeling the awkwardness of the moment. Again, the boy looked to the bishop, who indicated he needed to start once more.

After yet another flawed attempt, the new priest made it through the entire prayer. He stood and began passing trays to the deacons, who offered the sacred emblems to the waiting members. Some had perhaps grown impatient and felt a bit perturbed. After all, how hard is it to simply read a short paragraph? Why did this young man have to make such a production out of it and waste time that should go to the speakers?

But most in the congregation were probably not so harsh. In fact, many brethren could remember when they had made similar mistakes.

I cannot be sure what others thought during that prolonged sacrament prayer. However, I was quite moved by the experience. My friend Brett Sanders once pointed out to me that in such a moment we learn a great deal about the Savior's Atonement. The sacrament prayers must be offered word for word. The bishop has the responsibility to verify that they are spoken flawlessly. So what happened when this boy didn't get it right? Was he replaced, ridiculed, or rejected? No. That's not the Savior's way. But did the bishop just overlook the problem? No. He couldn't. The Lord requires the prayers to be perfect.

If the law of justice were the only law in force, then one slip-up, one wrong word by even the best-intentioned priesthood holder would have disqualified us all. Fortunately, the law of mercy was also in force. Although the sacramental prayers had to be perfect, and *that expectation could not be lowered*, the priest was given a second chance, and a third—as many times as it took. There was no trapdoor that opened up once he had gone too far. The bishop simply nodded and the young priesthood holder started over until he finally got the prayer right. No matter how many mistakes were made and corrected along the way, the final outcome was counted as perfect and acceptable.

God, like the bishop, cannot lower the standard that we ultimately become perfect (see Matthew 5:48; 3 Nephi 12:48), but He can give us many opportunities to start again. Like the young priest, we are all given the time we need to correct our mistakes. Perfection is our long-term goal, but for now our goal is progress in that direction—continuous progress that is possible only through the continuous Atonement.

Christ commanded us to forgive others seventy times seven times (see Matthew 18:22). Why is it so hard for us to believe He would forgive us more than once?

Time and time again He saves,
Forgiving my mistakes,

Seventy times seven times—
However long it takes.
(Steven Kapp Perry, "I Take His Name")

When I was serving as the bishop of a BYU ward, a young man came to me to confess, and I mean *confess*. He unloaded everything he had ever done wrong since elementary school. I heard what he had never had the courage to tell another bishop, stake president, mission president, or parent. While the sins were not of major proportions, they needed to be confessed and should have been taken care of years earlier. You can imagine the young man's relief and joy as he finally let go of all he had been carrying so needlessly and privately for so long. We prayed and reviewed some scriptures together. We discussed the role of confession in the repentance process and set goals for the future. When that young man left my office he almost floated out of the room.

The following Sunday I looked for him in church, but didn't see him. The next week he wasn't there either. I called his apartment and left messages. Finally I went over. The young man answered the door but didn't invite me in. His countenance was dark. His eyes were hollow. His comments were negative and sarcastic, revealing his depression. I asked if I could come in and talk with him.

He said, "Like that will make any difference." His words were cold and hard. "Just face it, Bishop, the Church isn't true. No one can even prove there is a God. It's all just a joke, so don't waste your time."

Wow! From floating on air to the pit of despair—and all in a matter of days. My first reaction was to become angry. He had no reason to be treating me so rudely. Next, I wanted to defend the truthfulness of the Church and the existence of God. Instead, I had one of those bishop moments: I knew what was wrong. Rather than raising my voice or quoting scripture, I simply said, "You messed up again, didn't you?"

His darkened expression melted, and this young returned missionary began to cry. Between sobs he motioned me into his empty apartment, where we sat together on the couch. He said, "Bishop, I'm sorry. I just feel so bad. I finally repented. I was finally clean. I finally put it all behind me. I finally used the Atonement, and it felt so good. Then I blew it all over again. Now my former sins have returned, and I feel like the worst person in the world."

I asked, "So the Church is true and there is a God after all?"

"Of course," he responded sheepishly.

"So you just need another chance?"

"But that's the problem. D&C 58:43: 'By this ye may know if a man repenteth of his sins—behold, he will confess them and forsake them.' I confessed; I didn't forsake. So I didn't really repent. It's over."

"Tell me about the Savior's grace, then."

He said, "Oh, you know—2 Nephi 25:23: 'It is by grace that we are saved, after all we can do.' We do our best and then Christ makes up the difference. But I did that, and it didn't work. I still went out and did the same old dumb thing. I blew it. Nothing changed."

I said, "Hold on. What do you mean Christ *makes up* the difference?"

He responded, "Well, just that. You have to do your best, and once you have done your best, Christ makes up the difference."

"Christ doesn't just make *up* the difference," I said. "He makes *all* the difference. He requires us to repent, but not as part of paying justice—only as part of helping us to change."

The young man said, "I thought it was like buying a bike. I pay all I can and then Jesus pays the rest."

I said, "I love Brother Stephen Robinson's parable (see *Believing Christ*, 30–32). He has helped us all see that there are two essential parts that must be completed in order for the Atonement to be fully effective in our lives. But I think of the Atonement more like this: Jesus already bought the whole bike. The few coins He asks from me are not so much to help pay for the bike, but rather to help me appreciate it, value it, and use it correctly."

The returned missionary said, "Either way, it doesn't matter since I just crashed the bike—so much for grace!"

I said, "Wait. What do you mean *so much for grace?* How can you give up so quickly? You think this is just a one-shot deal? Don't you realize Jesus has a whole garage full of bikes? Christ makes *all* the difference, and that means *all* the time. The miracle of the Atonement is that He will forgive our sins (plural). That includes not just multiple sins, but also multiple times we commit the same sin."

The young man said, "Are you saying it's okay to just sin and repent as often as I want?"

"Of course not. We don't condone sin. Joseph Smith taught clearly that 'repentance is a thing that cannot be trifled with everyday' (*Teachings*, 148). But the same Jesus who forgives those who 'know not what they do' (Luke 23:34) also stands ready to forgive those of us who know exactly what we do and just can't seem to stop (see Romans 3:23)."

The young man's face began to show hints of a smile. "So you're saying there is still hope for me."

"Now you are beginning to understand grace."

There is always hope in Christ (see 1 Corinthians 15:19; D&C 38:14–15). We hear many words associated with the Atonement: *infinite*, *eternal*, *everlasting*, *perfect*, *supreme*, *divine*, *incomprehensible*, *inexplicable*, even *personal* and *individual*. However, there is another word that must be more closely associated with the Atonement if we are ever going to be able to maintain hope in a world full of addictions, and that word is *continuous*—the continuous Atonement.

In *Preach My Gospel* we read, "Ideally, repenting of a specific sin should be necessary only once. However, if the sin is repeated, repentance is available as a means of healing (see Mosiah 26:30; Moroni 6:8; D&C 1:31–32). Repentance may involve an emotional and physical process. . . . Thus, both repentance and recovery may take time" (187–88).

Perhaps as we reflect on our lives, it is easy to convince ourselves we have sinned too often and gone too far to deserve the Atonement. We criticize ourselves harshly and beat ourselves up mercilessly. Perhaps we feel we have stepped beyond the reach of the Atonement by knowingly repeating a previously forsaken sin. We understand that God and Jesus were willing to forgive the first time, but we wonder how many more times they will be willing to watch us bumble along before they finally roll their eyes and declare, "Enough already!" We struggle so much to forgive ourselves that we wrongly assume God must be having the same struggle.

One young man wrote me the following e-mail: "I hate the fact that I am writing to you right now. But I knew that if I didn't I would feel much worse. I fell last night—again. Only this time it was much worse than ever before, for I am now a member of the higher priesthood. I had repented. I was clean. I swore that when I was ordained I would never again fall. Right now I feel like I have been given a gift and broken it into a million pieces. I feel sick inside. I have no appetite. I am so sick and tired of fighting with myself. I know I should not hate myself, but at the moment it is really hard not to do."

Another person wrote, "I really want to stop and every time I mess up I think, *Considering how bad I feel right now, I know I'll never mess up again*. And then I do. I have probably gone through that cycle about a thousand times. Everyone says I have to believe Christ, and not just believe in Him. Well, I do believe Him. It's just that He can't ever believe me. I sincerely and earnestly promise that my sins are over and they never really are. How many times can Christ watch this cycle without feeling like I am ridiculing His Atonement?"

Christ Himself answers, "As often as my people repent will I forgive them their trespasses against me" (Mosiah 26:30; see also Moroni 6:8). Would Christ command us to "continue to minister" to the afflicted (3 Nephi 18:32) if He were not willing to continually minister to us in our afflictions?

Even when we may not have completely forsaken a sin (see D&C 58:42–43), each time we repent we are one step closer to that goal—perhaps much closer than we think. Paul wrote, "Now is our salvation nearer than when we believed" (Romans 13:11). When we're tempted to give up, we must remember God is long-suffering, change is a process, and repentance is a pattern in our lives.

GOD IS LONG-SUFFERING

The divine attribute of long-suffering is a hard concept for time-bound mortals to grasp. We understand goodness, love, kindness, and forgiveness because we know people who demonstrate those godly qualities. However, even the nicest people have their limits.

God and Christ also have ultimate limits, but those final judgments are a long, long way down the road. We are not even close to reaching them. In the meantime, God and Jesus, who are not bound by clocks or calendars, can truly be long-suffering in a way we don't comprehend. Jesus says His "hand is stretched out *still*" (2 Nephi 19:12, 17, 21; emphasis added) and "Let not your heart be troubled, neither let it be afraid" (John 14:27). He who fed thousands with only a few loaves and fishes (see John 6:10–13) will certainly not run out of desire or ability to help us. He who rushed to the side of Lazarus (see John 12:2) will not slow down in His efforts to reach us. He who came to sleeping Apostles multiple times (see Mark 14:37–40) will not rest until we have also been revived.

At the end of his mission, one elder wrote, "I've learned that the fight in this life is not with others, but with ourselves. I've learned about the Atonement and that it can't be used up. It doesn't run out or expire. There is nothing on it that says, 'Best if used by this date.' It will always be a force in our lives."

Peter warned in graphic terms about returning to former sins when he wrote of dogs turning again to their own vomit and sows wallowing aimlessly in their mire (see 2 Peter 2:22). However, in the very next chapter Peter reminds us that God measures time differently than we do (see 2 Peter 3:8), and states that if we are diligent we "may be found of Him in peace, without spot, and blameless." It appears even habit-ridden dogs and sows can trust "that the longsuffering of our Lord is salvation" (2 Peter 3:14–15).

Bible translator William Tyndale (the man who gave us the English word *Atonement)* said, "If through fragility we fall a thousand times in a day, yet if we do repent again, we have alway mercy laid up for us in store in Jesus Christ our Lord" (in Wilcox, *Fire in the Bones*, 101). We see the Lord's long-suffering in how often early Apostles sent letters to the Saints, how frequently heavenly messengers came to Joseph Smith, and how regularly general conference happens in our day.

Perhaps there is no better example of the Lord's long-suffering than to remember how often prophets have been sent into this dark and sinful world. In Moroni 10:3 we read, "Remember how merciful the Lord hath been unto the children of men, from the creation of Adam even down until the time that ye shall receive these things." Throughout all history, whenever God's children have slipped into apostasy, prophets have been sent. Truly the Lord is saying, "I'll never, no never; I'll never, no never, no never forsake!" ("How Firm a Foundation," *Hymns*, no. 85).

CHANGE IS A PROCESS

Some say it is wrong to require change in others or in ourselves—that we should just accept everyone as is. Although kind and tolerant, this advice goes against both the upward reach within us and the teachings of Jesus Christ. Some of the most miserable people I know are those who have "accepted themselves" as they are and refuse to change. They have sought comfort in erasing the need for change rather than turning to heaven for help and realizing they get lots of chances to change and start again.

Realizing that change is a process, most of us would never get angry at a seed for not being a flower or expect a sculptor to transform a block of marble into a masterpiece overnight. In each case, we acknowledge the potential and patiently hope for and nurture the development.

Alma taught that developing faith in Christ, the first principle of the gospel, was like the process of planting a seed and watching it grow. The second principle, repentance, is no less a process. King Lamoni's father proclaimed, "I will give away all my sins to know thee" (Alma 22:18), and experienced a dramatic change. Most of us find the giving away of our sins takes more time.

Elder D. Todd Christofferson testified, "The remarkable examples . . . in scripture are just that—remarkable and not typical. For most of us, the changes are more gradual and occur over time" ("Born Again," 78). We must be careful not to speak of being born again as if it always happens in an instant (see 2 Corinthians 5:17; Mosiah 27:25–29; Alma 7:14). Why would our spiritual rebirth be any less a process than our physical birth? Doctors and nurses record the exact minute of a birth, but ask the mother who carried the baby and endured labor how long the process really took. Our spiritual rebirth takes even longer.

Although scriptures offer stern warnings for those who procrastinate their repentance (see Helaman 13:38; Alma 13:27), there is a big difference between procrastinating the day of our repentance and working through a repentance process, which more often than not takes more than a day. It is the difference between saying, "I'll repent one day down the road" and actually spending many days *on* the road. There is no "right time" for which we have to wait to repent. There are many right times all along the way. Elder Neal A. Maxwell wrote, "This is a gospel of grand expectations, but God's grace is sufficient for each of us if we remember that there are no instant Christians" (*Notwithstanding* My *Weakness*, 11).

Little children don't learn to walk in a day. Between the

time a child is carried in a parent's arms and the great day when he is running on his own, there is a lot of hand holding, baby stepping, and falling. For a child learning to walk, falling down may not be desirable, but the lessons learned from it are.

Similarly, before we came to the world, God knew we had progressed as far as we were able without an earthly experience. He could no longer carry us by keeping us in His presence. It was time for His children to learn how to walk on their own. That's why He lovingly placed us here—across the room, so to speak—and stepped just beyond our reach, all the while beckoning us to come. He knew the tumbles that awaited us. He knew the ups and downs ahead. That's why He planned from the very start to send our older brother to hold our hands, lift us up, and guide us across the room back to His outstretched arms. We left those arms crawling. We can return to them running.

Most of us are familiar with the scripture in Ether 12:27, which teaches that we are given weakness to ensure humility and that Christ's grace is sufficient to make weak things strong. But it seems we expect that transition to be instantaneous. Christ could change us with a wave of His hand, but He knows that strength too easily achieved is not valued or enduring. That's why as He changes weaknesses into strengths He usually uses the same natural process of a child learning to walk—one foot in front of another, one day after another, and even one fall after another.

We know that God cannot "look upon sin with the least degree of allowance" (Alma 45:16; D&C 1:31), and that "all have sinned" (Romans 3:23), so what chance do any of us have? The answer is a second chance, a third chance, a fourth chance—as many as we need to get it right. God, who cannot look on sin with the least degree of allowance, can lovingly look on repentant sinners with a great deal of allowance and patience. He knows that change is necessary, and through Christ's Atonement it is possible, but it is usually evolutionary rather than revolutionary.

God "doth not dwell in unholy temples" (Alma 7:21), but isn't His spirit still felt in temples that are under construction or being remodeled? Building a temple takes years. The earth was formed in six creative periods (see Moses 2). Enoch's Zion became a perfect society "in process of time" (Moses 7:21). Moses and Alma were translated after years of sanctification (see Alma 45:19). It appears even those who end up in the celestial kingdom will still be engaged in the perfecting process, for we read in D&C 76:60 that "they *shall* overcome all things" (emphasis added) and not that they already have. This life is the time to prepare to meet God (see Alma 12:24), but we still have eternity to learn to be like Him.

REPENTANCE IS A PATTERN

In Joseph Smith's earliest account of his youthful experience in the Sacred Grove, he stressed that he had sought for and obtained forgiveness of his sins (see Backman, *Joseph Smith's First Vision*, 206–8). Yet over the next three years Joseph felt remorse over "foolish errors," "weakness[es] of youth," and "foibles of human nature" (Joseph Smith–History 1:28). Consequently, he retired to his bed and poured out his heart to God seeking forgiveness. It was at this time that Moroni first visited him. It appears that even in the life of the Prophet, asking for and receiving forgiveness was not just a one-time experience. Seeing God, Jesus, and angels did not make Joseph immune from "sins and follies." Revelations often contained chastisements and solemn warnings, but how comforting it must have been for him to also hear the phrase, "Your sins are forgiven you." How comforting it is for us to see how often he and others heard that same reassuring phrase throughout many subsequent years (see D&C 29:3; 36:1; 50:36; 60:7; 62:3; 64:3; 84:61).

President Boyd K. Packer called sincere repentance a pattern in our lives (see "Brilliant Morning of Forgiveness," 7). On another occasion, he testified that even "an ordinary soul—struggling against temptation, failing and repenting, and failing again and repenting, but always determined to keep [his] covenants" can still expect to one day hear "Well done, thou good and faithful servant" (*Let Not Your Heart Be Troubled*, 257).

At a BYU Women's Conference, Janet Lee said: "Christ healed bodies, minds, and souls. But after he healed the lepers, were they free from other struggles? After he restored sight to the blind, were they free from fear? Were the five thousand Christ fed ever hungry again? Was the sea calmed by Christ's hand stirred by future storms? Yes" ("Pieces of Peace," 10). Our needs—including the need for forgiveness—are continuous, and so is Christ's Atonement in its ability to meet those needs.

Perhaps the most amazing lesson to be learned from Christ's many miracles is that to Him, they were not miraculous. They were commonplace occurrences in His life. As repentance becomes a regular pattern in our lives, we come to appreciate more and more that offering forgiveness is a regular pattern in His.

So, the next time a young man reading the sacrament prayer makes a mistake, remember, that's what the sacrament is all about. That's what the continuous Atonement is all about—giving us the chance to begin again. How many times? Seventy times seven times—however long it takes.

Chapter 2

WHO NEEDS A SAVIOR?

We would never dream of separating the symbols of the Atonement by taking the bread without the water or vice versa when partaking of the sacrament. Together they teach us of immortality and eternal life. Neither one without the other is a whole gift. Both are required to truly make us whole.

When Joseph and Mary announced that the name of their son would be Jesus, it probably, like many other unique circumstances associated with His birth, raised some eyebrows. Shouldn't the child be given the name of His father, as was tradition? Little did the questioning crowds know that *for precisely that reason* the baby would not be named Joseph. Jesus' real Father was God, who sent an angel to declare that the child's name would be Jesus—the Greek translation of the Hebrew *Jeshua*, meaning *God is help* or *Savior*.

Latter-day Saints are far from being the only ones who call Jesus the Savior. I have known people from many denominations who say those words with great feeling and deep emotion. After hearing one such passionate declaration from a devoutly Christian friend, I asked, "From what did Jesus save us?"

My friend was taken aback by the question, and struggled to answer. He spoke of having a personal relationship with Jesus and being born again. He spoke of his intense love and endless gratitude for the Savior, but he still never gave a clear answer to the question.

I contrast that experience with a visit to an LDS Primary where I asked the same question: "If a Savior saves, from what did Jesus save us?"

One child answered, "From the bad guys."

Another said, "He saved us from getting really, really, hurt really, really bad."

Still another added, "He opened up the door so we can live again after we die and go back to heaven."

Then one bright future missionary explained, "Well, it's like this—there are two deaths, see, physical and spiritual, and Jesus, well, he just beat the pants off both of them." Although their language was far from refined, these children showed a clear understanding of how their Savior has saved them.

Jesus did indeed overcome the two deaths that came in consequence of the Fall of Adam and Eve. Because Jesus Christ "hath abolished death, and hath brought life and immortality to light" (2 Timothy 1:10), we will all overcome physical death by being resurrected and obtaining immortality.

Because Jesus overcame spiritual death caused by sin—Adam's and our own—we all have the opportunity to repent, be cleansed, and live with our Heavenly Father and other loved ones eternally. "Though your sins be as scarlet, they shall be as white as snow" (Isaiah 1:18). To Latter-day Saints this knowledge is basic and fundamental—a lesson learned in Primary. We are blessed to have such an understanding.

I remember a man in Chile who scoffed, "Who needs a Savior?" Apparently he didn't yet understand the precariousness and limited duration of his present state. President Ezra Taft Benson wrote: "Just as a man does not really desire food until he is hungry, so he does not desire the salvation of Christ until he knows why he needs Christ. No one adequately and properly knows why he needs Christ until he understands and accepts the doctrine of the Fall and its effects upon all mankind" ("Book of Mormon," 85).

Perhaps the man who asked, "Who needs a Savior?" would ask President Benson, "Who believes in Adam and Eve?" Like many who deny significant historical events, perhaps he thinks Adam and Eve are only part of a folktale. Perhaps he has never heard of them before. Regardless of whether or not this man accepts the Fall, he still faces its effects.

If this man has not yet felt the sting of death and sin, he will. Sooner or later someone close to him will die, and he will know the awful emptiness and pain of feeling as if part of his soul is being buried right along with the body of his loved one. On that day, he will hurt in a way he has not yet experienced. He will need a Savior.

Similarly, sooner or later, he will feel guilt, remorse, and shame for his sins. He will finally run out of escape routes and have to face himself in the mirror knowing full well that his selfish choices have affected others as well as himself. On that day, he will hurt in a profound and desperate way. He will need a Savior. And Christ will be there to save from both the sting of death and the stain of sin.

THE STING OF DEATH

Of the 62,000 people who attended the open house following the remodeling of the temple in Santiago, Chile, one was a father who supported his wife and children in their desires to participate in the Church but resisted being baptized himself. I had met the father several times previously, so when he finished the temple tour I couldn't resist teasing him a little. "Did you see the chair?" I asked.

He responded, "What chair?"

I said, "The one with your name on it. The one that is in there waiting for you to get baptized so you can bring your family back to the temple to be sealed."

He smiled and chuckled good-naturedly. "Oh, President Wilcox," he said, "my life is just fine as it is. You can take my name off that chair. I don't need it."

A few months later his "just fine" life changed drastically. His sixteen-year-old son, a priest, was out riding his bicycle around the neighborhood when a gang stopped him and demanded the bike. He wasn't about to give it up without a fight, so his attackers pulled a knife and stabbed the defenseless teenager to death.

When the father heard of his son's murder, he was so overcome with anger and hate that he set out immediately in search of the gang members, but he did not find them. At night his grief was inconsolable. His tears could not be stopped. He found little relief in sleep because nightmares haunted him. For the first time in his life he was forced to think seriously about death, and seemingly unanswerable questions taunted him. Was his son really gone forever? Were these few short years really all he had? Was everything the boy had learned and done for nothing? Did this teenager go through all the experiences of growing up just to end in a grave? This father knew his son was good and had influenced many lives with his example. The father knew of the bright and promising future the boy had once had ahead of him. Could such great potential go unrealized? Friends told him that his boy would live on in his memory, but that brought little comfort. Who would remember his son when he too was gone? This man who had claimed he didn't need a Savior was now slapped in the face with the stark reality of our fallen condition.

A modern philosopher once wrote, "This is the terror; to have emerged from nothing, to have a name, consciousness of self, deep inner feelings, an excruciating inner yearning for life, and self-expression—and with all this yet to die. It seems like a hoax" (in Nibley, "Not to Worry," 151).

Similarly Joseph Smith asked, "What is the object of our coming into existence, then dying and falling away, to be here no more?" (*History of the Church*, 6:50). But then Joseph Smith proceeded to do something others had not: He provided answers. And these answers were exactly what this Chilean father desperately craved.

The man requested to meet with the missionaries. As they taught him, a measure of peace began to replace despair; a measure of hope began to replace hate. Soon, I was honored to be invited to attend his baptism.

When I saw him enter the room dressed in white, I greeted him with a warm *abrazo*. I'll never forget the intensity in his voice as he spoke in my ear, "Is it still there? Is the chair with my name on it still waiting for me in the temple?"

I hugged him again. Who could even begin to imagine all he had suffered? "Yes," I assured him. "The chair is still there.

As you stay faithful and prepare, in one year you will be able to enter the temple and be sealed to your family—your whole family."

The man who only a few months before had told me he was "just fine" had found out how desperately he needed a Savior. And Jesus was there for him, just as He is for all of us.

THE STAIN OF SIN

Along with physical death, the consequences of sin, or spiritual death, must also be faced. One day a missionary called and asked if I would interview a woman for baptism. She needed the additional interview because the young district leader who had done the first interview had dutifully asked her if she had ever participated in an abortion, and she had answered yes.

When I met with her, she tearfully told me details of her past she had never shared before with anyone. As a young bride she had become pregnant. She was joyful, but her husband was furious. He scolded her and demanded she get an abortion. He claimed they could not afford a baby. When she refused, he beat her severely and promised that the beatings would continue until she agreed. For her self-preservation, she finally conceded, but she never forgave her husband or herself.

Years later the marriage ended in ruins. The husband's drinking and unfaithfulness had brought this woman nothing but heartache. On her own she sought a better life, yet she still carried the constant memory of the baby she had given up. Through her tears, she said, "There is not a day that passes that

I don't think about how old my child would be now and what my child would be doing. There is not a day that passes that I don't privately beg for forgiveness from my child and from God."

No one knew about this woman's private prayers. Even her closest relatives were unaware of the abortion or the sorrow that followed it. When she met the missionaries she found new hope as they taught her of Jesus and the Atonement. They spoke of baptism and the chance to be cleansed, but it seemed too good to be true. She convinced herself they were only making such a promise because they didn't know of her dark deed.

As my interview with her concluded, she said, "Now that you know, I am sure you will tell me I am not worthy to be baptized."

"On the contrary," I said. "With all my heart I testify that through the Atonement of Jesus Christ you can be forgiven, cleansed, and made totally whole again." I explained that the consequence of the choice could not be changed, but the pain she felt could be replaced with peace.

She smiled sweetly and said, "President Wilcox, you have no idea how much I wish I could believe you, but I really don't think there is anything that can make me clean again. I am afraid that if I got baptized God would curse me for daring to enter such holy water unworthily." We both left the interview downhearted.

Several days later she requested another meeting. In this interview she told me of a dream in which she was dressed in white ready to be baptized, but when she approached the font it was filled with white flowers instead of water. "What does it mean?" she asked. "What is God saying?"

I responded, "Perhaps this is His way of telling you to not be afraid of baptism. He wants you to be baptized so you can become as clean as those white flowers."

Together we read the words of Jesus in 3 Nephi 9:13: "Return unto me, and repent of your sins, and be converted, that I may heal you." I explained, "Perhaps the miraculous physical healings performed by the Savior on relatively few people stand as tangible reminders of the greatest healing He offers all people—the healing of our sick and sin-stained souls" (see McConkie, Millet, and Top, *Doctrinal Commentary*, 4:41). I suggested when she felt unworthy she could close her eyes and picture Jesus' resurrected body, which, though perfect, still carried the marks of His crucifixion. I said, "He has chosen to retain His scars to remind us that we can be rid of ours." She thought about that image for a moment and then committed to be baptized the next weekend. I arranged my schedule to attend the service.

My customary gift for new members was a book to aid them in their gospel study. However, this time was different. Along with a book, I brought flowers—a bouquet of fresh, clean, beautiful white flowers. She held them throughout the entire meeting.

No one attending realized how many years she had carried the grief, shame, and remorse that accompanied her private decision. No one else knew about her dream and why the white flowers meant so much to her. She knew how much she needed a Savior. And Jesus was there for her, just as He is for all of us.

NOT ONE WITHOUT THE OTHER

Latter-day Saints testify to the entire world that Jesus saves us from death by offering immortality, and from sin by offering eternal life (see Moses 1:39). In addition, He also saves us from obtaining one without the other.

When my daughter Whitney was in fourth grade, she read a wonderful book called *Tuck Everlasting* by Natalie Babbitt. The book tells of a family who drinks from the fountain of youth and then discovers that living forever does not bring them the happiness they had imagined. Instead of spreading the good news about the secret spring, they devote their immortality to protecting others from their fate.

One night Whitney said, "Daddy, I have a question. You know how you always said that because of Jesus we will live forever?"

I could see the wheels turning in her mind as I answered, "Yes."

She asked, "What if I don't want to?"

I felt grateful to be able to explain to my wonderful fourth-grade daughter that immortality is only part of Jesus' gift.

On its own, immortality may not be such a desirable prize. Even young Whitney realized that eternity is a pretty long time. Studies suggest that most people across the world believe we are going to some kind of heaven, but to do what? If immortality were all that Christ offered, I, like my daughter, may want to consider other options.

If heaven offers no promise of being with those I love, what kind of heaven is that? If it offers me no chance for development, no chance to use all I have learned through this earthly school to help others progress, I would be unsure about wanting to go.

Thankfully, Jesus did not limit us to a partial gift, a half gift, a box with pretty wrapping and nothing inside. Jesus gave us a full and whole salvation of immortality complete with the possibility of eternal progression. There will always be something more to look forward to and achieve. As my mom, Val C. Wilcox, once wrote:

> *For the eager intellect,*
> *The learner with more interests than hours,*
> *Eternity promises to be*
> *Heaven indeed.*

After Adam and Eve partook of the fruit of the tree of knowledge of good and evil, God set guards over the tree of life. There had to be two trees—real options with real consequences. God gave our first parents freedom to choose, and he meant it. Life is not a simulator. It is the real thing. Still, in His mercy, He sent angels and a flaming sword to point Adam and Eve away from the fruit that would have let them live forever (see Moses 4:31; Alma 42:3). Why? Didn't He want them to live forever? Of course He did, but not *in their sins*. Had they partaken of that fruit, then just like the fictional Tucks who drank of the fountain of youth, Adam and Eve would have lived forever without the possibility of eternal progression. So God steered them away from that possibility with a flaming sword—not a symbol of God's anger, justice, or punishment, but a symbol of His love pointing the way toward Christ's Atonement. In the glow of that flaming sword Adam and Eve—and ultimately all of us—find both of Christ's gifts.

Just as immortality without the possibility of eternal life would be incomplete, so the celestial kingdom would be undesirable if there were a time limit attached. It would be a cruel God indeed who would take us clear through a premortal existence, this earth life, and all yet to come in the future and then announce that heaven will not last or that we must simply start the process over again. Eternal life—life with God and loved ones—without the promise of immortality would be nothing more than a continuation of the pain of mortality, an existence darkened by the knowledge that all good things must eventually end. Tears of happiness shed at temple weddings would become bitter tears if the never-ending images reflected in temple mirrors did not represent an eternal reality and our treasured relationships couldn't continue.

We would never dream of separating the symbols of the Atonement by taking the bread without the water or vice versa when partaking of the sacrament. Together they teach us of immortality *and* eternal life. Neither one without the other is a whole gift. Both are required to truly make us whole.

EVERY KNEE SHALL BOW

For now, Latter-day Saints are among the few who know these truths, but one day everyone will. Scriptures promise that every knee will bow and every tongue confess that Jesus is the Christ and that our immortality and eternal life are thanks to Him (see Isaiah 45:23; Romans 14:11; Mosiah 27:31; D&C 88:104). Just as it was with my friends in Chile, many may not realize it now, but sooner or later we must all face the question posed by Pilate: "What shall I do then with Jesus which is called Christ?" (Matthew 27:22).

Sadly, millions do not know the first thing about Him. Others may know of Him, but remain indifferent or blind to His influence and gifts. Still others knowingly disobey His commandments and ridicule that which is sacred. For them Jesus is nothing more than a swear word or the punch line of a joke.

I once sat several rows in front of two men in a plane bound for Salt Lake City. One said to the other, "Do you think we ought to go see the blankity-blank Mormon temple?"

The other responded, "You idiot. They won't let you in the blankity-blank temple. You have to go to a blankity-blank visitors' center." He then proceeded to tell a "funny" story about how he and another buddy had once visited there and seen the statue of Christ with His arms extended. Instead of being moved spiritually, these two plotted about how they might be able to tie a yo-yo to Jesus' finger and take a picture without getting caught.

I was sick as I listened to these men talk so sacrilegiously.

They, like the Roman soldiers who nailed Jesus to the cross, "know not what they do" (Luke 23:34). Like the people in Enoch's day, their "hearts have waxed hard, and their ears are dull of hearing, and their eyes cannot see afar off" (Moses 6:27). It seems the people described by John are not the only ones who do not know they are "wretched, and miserable, and poor, and blind" (Revelation 3:17). Sadly, what Christ "finished" on the cross (John 19:30) has not yet begun to matter in far too many lives.

Consider the following snapshots:

1. A non-LDS friend told me how when she first moved into her home, neighbors met her with cans of beer in their hands and announced they were Mormons.
2. In Chile I met many young people named Mosiah, Nephi, and Moroni who had never set foot in an LDS chapel and were covered with tattoos and body piercings.
3. My students have pointed out essays posted on the Internet written by graduates of Brigham Young University who are now living alternative lifestyles and ridiculing the very honor code they once signed and the Church for which they once served missions.

Do such members give the Church a "bad name"? Of course they do. Nevertheless, I like to think they also highlight the *need* for the Church of Jesus Christ and emphasize how totally dependent we *all* are on the baby who was not named Joseph.

WHAT WE CAN OFFER HIM

For as many as there are who reject Him, there are others who stay true. In the hearts of many faithful disciples there is no question why or whether they need Christ. Their private doubt is whether He needs them. The Firstborn in the premortal existence, the Creator of the universe, the worker of miracles and greatest of us all—does He need them? He does.

For members of Christ's Church, the bread of the sacrament represents Christ's body, the water His blood. But without us, those blessed emblems merely sit in trays. We must pick them up and put them inside. We must internalize Jesus' offering. That's how we thank Jesus for all He has done—by accepting His love, remembering His sacrifice, and applying His teachings and Atonement in our lives. Christ's gifts are freely given, but they must also be freely received (see D&C 88:33).

Mistakenly we think that Jesus already has everything, but He doesn't. He doesn't have you. He doesn't have me—not until we give ourselves to Him. Elder Bruce C. Hafen wrote: "The Lord cannot save us without our own good-faith effort . . . no matter how much He would give to make us His. . . . He not only would not, He cannot control us against our will" (*Believing Heart*, 85). Elder Neal A. Maxwell confirmed this truth when he taught, "The submission of one's will is really the only uniquely personal thing we have to place on God's altar" ("Swallowed Up," 24).

The word *atonement* is often broken up so it reads *at-one-ment*, but there is another word found among the letters that also could and must be emphasized—*me*. Not only did Christ do it all for me but He also anxiously waits for me to accept it, to internalize it, and to make it count.

As insignificant as I sometimes feel, I still have something to offer Him—the same thing my children offer me as a father. When my daughter Whitney was small, she said, "Dad, you are a hard worker."

I said, "It's how I take care of you."

She replied, "I'm sorry. If you never had me, you would not have to work so hard."

I wrapped her in my arms and said, "If I never had you, my life would be empty. Working hard is a small price to pay to have you." She then gave me a spontaneous and heartfelt hug that filled me with joy.

When my teenage son David slid a note under my bedroom door thanking me and expressing love, I felt that same joy. When my oldest son, Russell, was sealed to his wife, Trish, in the temple, and when my oldest daughter, Wendee, shared her testimony at BYU Women's Conference, I was once again filled with joy.

That is what Alma felt when the belief and faith of those he was teaching caused him to declare, "Great is my joy" (Alma 7:17). That is the same feeling we can offer Christ when we show we feel confident in His care. As we remember, value, and honor the father of our rebirth, we give Him joy in His posterity.

Jesus doesn't need followers to give Him self-esteem, authority, or power. He stands supreme completely independent of followers. However, He does receive from disciples something that all the esteem, authority, and power in the universe cannot offer: joy. In the Old World, Christ counseled His followers to keep the commandments and to love one another. "These things have I spoken unto you," He said, "that *your* joy may be full" (John 15:10–12; emphasis added). However, when He came to the Americas and saw the faithfulness, love, and acceptance of the people, He declared, "And now behold, *my* joy is full" (3 Nephi 17:20; emphasis added).

Announcing Christ's birth, the angel declared, "I bring you good tidings of great joy" (Luke 2:10). Jesus' life and sacrifice bring joy to us, and our coming to Him can and will bring similar joy to Him. I find profound purpose in knowing that in that one small, personal way He "needs" me. "Men are, that they might have joy" (2 Nephi 2:25), but men are also that they might give joy to Him. Imagine how He will feel when He can finish in a different way the sorrowful plea He made so long ago: "How often would I have gathered [you] together, even as a hen gathereth her chickens under her wings, and ye *would*" (Matthew 23:37; emphasis added).

Elder Bruce C. Hafen wrote: "Christ's Atonement is at the very core of [God's] plan. Without His dear, dear sacrifice, there would be no way home, no way to be together, no way to be like Him. He gave us all *He* had. Therefore, 'how great is his joy' (D&C 18:13) when even one of us 'gets it'—when we look up from the weed patch and turn our face to the Son" ("The Atonement: All for All," 98).

We read that "the glory of God is intelligence" (D&C

93:36). What am I, in my purest form, but an organized intelligence? (see Abraham 3:22). Through my righteous choice to give myself to God and Jesus, I bring them glory (see D&C 132:31, 63). And in a world full of ignorance, apathy, and open rebellion, that offering matters. It may seem small. It may be limited, but it is not trivial because, simply put, our Heavenly Father and our Savior Jesus Christ grieve if we choose not to take advantage of the sacred Atonement in our lives.

When my mother taught second grade, a young girl became sick during class one day. Mom finally called the child's mother, who took her to the doctor and discovered that she had a serious and painful infection in both ears. The mother asked her daughter, "Why didn't you tell me it was this bad?"

The daughter said, "Because you would have made me stay home, and my teacher would have missed me!"

If we choose to stay behind, we will surely miss out, but our Father in Heaven will also miss us. Where there is great love and attachment, there is great risk of pain. God knew that from the start, but He loved us anyway. God's effectiveness and ultimate success as a parent is not dependent on us individually, but a measure of His personal joy is.

Christ offers victory over death and sin. However, the Resurrection will be a singular event, as will the final judgment. Those moments, as amazing as they will be, will come and go. Every knee bending and every tongue confessing may also be only a moment. But our ability to bring God joy is endless.

If I am not careful, the Atonement can be seen with an eye single to *my* glory because it takes care of *my* death and *my* sins.

As I see it with an eye single to God's glory, I realize that the Atonement is truly continuous. The continuous nature of the Atonement is found not only in Christ's complete gift, which we receive, but also in our discovering the gifts of heart and will that we have to give, and then offering them to God continuously.

Chapter 3

HE'S GOT US COVERED

The Fall was designed—complete with all the accompanying misery and pain—to ultimately bring us freedom and happiness. There is no shortcut to the celestial kingdom. Everyone who ends up there must pass through the lone and dreary world on the way. God knew the problems associated with a mortal probation, but He also knew that Jesus would be the solution to those problems.

We hear the words *Jesus* and *Christ* together so often, some mistakenly think *Christ* was Jesus' last name. During His lifetime Jesus was known as Jesus the carpenter or Jesus of Nazareth. We have surnames today that also denote a profession (like *Cook*) or place (like *Field*). *Christ* is not a surname. It is a title. It is the English form of the Greek *Cristos*, which is equivalent to the Hebrew *Messiah*, which means *The Anointed One*.

Long before we were born, and even before the Fall of Adam and Eve, Jesus was anointed by God the Father to be our Savior and Redeemer (see D&C 138:42). Those who do not understand the premortal existence cannot understand how Jesus was foreordained to His role. Some mistakenly think that God planned for this earth to be a perpetual Garden of Eden for everyone, that Adam and Eve could have managed to have children despite their state of innocence, and that the goal for humanity was to live forever picking flowers and frolicking with the animals. Those who hold this belief see Satan as one who ruined God's plan by tempting Adam and Eve. They claim that the choice to eat of the fruit was not in God's original plan, and then He had to undo the damage, to fix the problem, to plug the hole in the dam, in order to avoid certain disaster for Adam and Eve and their posterity. According to some, that was when

God decided to send Jesus to make the best of a bad situation. They teach that, while we can't thwart God's plan in the long run, we are currently experiencing a major setback. Although I've encountered this version of life's beginnings many times, I find it difficult to have faith and confidence in a God who is taking all of humanity on an alternate route that is less than His initial will for us.

For Latter-day Saints, God is all powerful and also all knowing (see 2 Nephi 9:20; Alma 26:35; Moroni 7:22). Our Father in Heaven has always known that we would grow and progress best in a telestial world rather than in a garden paradise. He knew Adam and Eve would not be able to bear and effectively raise children until they gained knowledge. God knew death was a necessary part of our eternal progression, and sin would be an inevitable result of being out of His presence with no memory of Him. He knew earth life would not be the end, but one more step in the right direction.

God allowed Satan to tempt Adam and Eve, all the while knowing that they would transgress and fall. Although they had to make this conscious choice for themselves, it was not against God's master plan or His wishes. Their fall wasn't down. Rather, as I have heard it expressed, they fell "forward."

Think of all Adam and Eve knew when they finally passed away that they hadn't known when they were in the Garden! "Their years of mortal experience with repentance, humility, sorrow, and faithful striving became the Lord's course of instruction to help Adam and Eve develop the capacity to live a meaningful celestial life" (Hafen and Hafen, *Belonging Heart*, 69).

The Fall was designed—complete with all the accompanying misery and pain—to ultimately bring us freedom and happiness. There is no shortcut to the celestial kingdom. Everyone who ends up there must pass through the lone and dreary world on the way. God knew the problems associated with a mortal probation, but He also knew that Jesus would be the solution to those problems. To that end Christ was anointed. Just as the Fall was necessary to overcome the blockade that stood between our premortal spirits and their eternal potential, the Atonement was necessary to overcome all effects of the Fall. Jesus would provide a way for us to be resurrected and, by His shouldering our punishment and guilt, a way to be cleansed. However, those would not be the end of His gifts. He also took upon Himself our infirmities and sorrows. He provided a way for us to be consoled through every trial. He suffered alone so that we would never have to do the same. Through His Atonement all of us can be covered, helped, comforted, and ultimately embraced.

TO BE COVERED

The English word *Atonement* comes from the ancient Hebrew word *kaphar,* which means *to cover.* When Adam and Eve partook of the fruit and discovered their nakedness in the Garden of Eden, God sent Jesus to make coats of skins to cover them. Coats of skins don't grow on trees. They had to be made from an animal, which meant an animal had to be killed. Perhaps that was the very first animal sacrifice. Because of that sacrifice, Adam and Eve were covered physically. In the same way, through Jesus' sacrifice we are also covered emotionally and spiritually. When Adam and Eve left the garden, the only things they could take to remind them of Eden were the coats of skins. The one physical thing we take with us out of the temple to remind us of *that* heavenly place is a similar covering. The garment reminds us of our covenants, protects us, and even promotes modesty. However, it is also a powerful and personal symbol of the Atonement—a continuous reminder both night and day that because of Jesus' sacrifice, we are covered. (I am indebted to Guinevere Woolstenhulme, a religion teacher at BYU, for insights about *kaphar*.)

Jesus covers us (see Alma 7) when we feel worthless and inadequate. Christ referred to Himself as "Alpha and Omega" (3 Nephi 9:18). *Alpha* and *omega* are the first and last letters of the Greek alphabet. Christ is surely the beginning and the end. Those who study statistics learn that the letter *alpha* is used to represent the level of significance in a research study. Jesus is also the one who gives value and significance to everything. Robert L. Millet writes, "In a world that offers flimsy and fleeting remedies for mortal despair, Jesus comes to us in our moments of need with a 'more excellent hope' (Ether 12:32)" (*Grace Works*, 62).

Jesus covers us when we feel lost and discouraged. Christ referred to Himself as the "light" (3 Nephi 18:16). He doesn't always clear the path, but He does illuminate it. Along with being the light, He also lightens our loads. "For my yoke is easy," He said, "and my burden is light" (Matthew 11:30). He doesn't always take burdens away from us, but He strengthens us for the task of carrying them and promises they will be for our good.

Jesus covers us when we feel abused and hurt. Joseph Smith taught that because Christ met the demands of justice, all injustices will be made right for the faithful in the eternal scheme of things (see *Teachings*, 296). Marie K. Hafen has said, "The gospel of Jesus Christ was not given us to prevent our pain. The gospel was given us to heal our pain" ("Eve Heard All These Things," 27).

Jesus covers us when we feel defenseless and abandoned. Christ referred to Himself as our "advocate" (D&C 29:5): one who believes in us and stands up to defend us. We read, "The Lord is my rock, and my fortress, and my deliverer; my God, my strength, in whom I will trust; my buckler" (Psalm 18:2). A buckler is a shield used to divert blows. Jesus doesn't always protect us from unpleasant consequences of illness or the choices of others, since they are all part of what we are here on earth to experience. However, He does shield us from fear in those dark times and delivers us from having to face those difficulties alone.

TO BE HELPED

A woman once asked, "Other than just being nice, why would Christ care about inadequacies, grief, sicknesses, and discouragement if such mortal experiences do not make us unclean?" Although they are not sins, many mortal experiences still have the potential to pull us far from God if not seen with the perspective provided by the plan of salvation. Too many raise an angry fist toward heaven and say, "Why me?" not realizing that in those very moments they need to extend an open hand toward heaven and plead for help.

John the Baptist prophesied, "Every valley shall be filled, and every mountain and hill shall be brought low" (Luke 3:4). Perhaps in the future those words will be literally fulfilled, but for now they describe figuratively the very real help Jesus offers. If the knuckles of our hands represent the valleys and mountains of our lives, it is Jesus who offers to hold our hands through both. If we but extend our hand to Him, He will take it. While many in the world see God's help as having about the same effect as a rabbit's foot or lucky charm, faithful Saints who make covenants with God in His holy house know the power that comes from feeling His hand in theirs. Truly, as John prophesied, Jesus makes every mountain manageable and fills every valley.

President Boyd K. Packer wrote: "For some reason, we think the Atonement of Christ applies *only* at the end of mortal life to redemption from the Fall, from spiritual death. It is much more than that. It is an ever-present power to call upon in everyday life. . . . The Atonement has practical, personal, [and] everyday value" ("Touch of the Master's Hand," 23–24; emphasis in original).

I remember attending the baptism of a wonderful middle-aged couple in Chile. Gloria and José had been taught by sister missionaries who introduced me to them as they prepared for baptism. I had seen other baptisms where refreshments were served, but never by the ones getting baptized. Gloria had made a cake and wanted to serve everyone herself. That was just her way. She had been very involved in the women's organization of her former church, and when she joined the Church of Jesus Christ she served in the Relief Society with even greater diligence.

"What is your fondest desire?" I once asked her.

She responded, "I want my children to see the light and also come into the Church." But her older children continued to tell their parents they had made a mistake by joining. Gloria would only smile and say, "You will see in time that we did the right thing."

Before long Gloria started to miss church meetings occasionally—not because of lack of desire, but because she was having a hard time walking. She assumed she was just getting older and it was naturally more difficult for her to move than it once had been. Despite the challenge, she struggled onward and redoubled her efforts.

Then one day, the sister missionaries called me with terrible news. Gloria had been diagnosed with ALS (amyotrophic lateral sclerosis), better known as Lou Gehrig's disease. This horrible, debilitating disease shuts down the body by slowly constricting movement, and ultimately ends in death. As the illness paralyzes the body, it leaves its victims totally alert and aware of what is happening. The sisters were beside themselves with worry. They explained, "Not only has this diagnosis come as a great shock to Gloria and José, but now the older children are telling them that this is God's punishment for joining the Mormon Church."

I wondered how a young and inexperienced doctor in one of the worst public hospitals in Santiago could have made such a serious diagnosis accurately with no tests whatsoever. I began inquiring about more qualified physicians and was given the name of the top specialist in the country, who worked at the finest hospital. I contacted him and explained the situation. He confirmed that ALS was difficult to diagnose in its early stages, and said it was much rarer in women than in men. I told the missionaries I felt Gloria needed to be tested before she accepted such a grim diagnosis, but they told me Gloria and José could never afford to see a specialist.

That's when the sister missionaries took action. On their own they began writing their family members and friends. They explained the situation and asked for help. They contacted former missionaries who had known Gloria and José before leaving their missions and asked for their help as well. Some of my own relatives heard of the situation and also volunteered assistance. When the donations were totaled there was more than enough to have Gloria tested by the top specialist in the country.

Imagine our disappointment when the diagnosis came back exactly the same. The first doctor had been right. After we left the specialist's office, Gloria looked at me, holding back the tears, and said, "At least we know for sure and can stop wondering."

José said, "President Wilcox, will you please give her a

blessing?" We found an empty room in the hospital and I blessed Gloria to replace her fears with faith.

The disease progressed more rapidly than anyone had anticipated. Though there is no cure, there are medicines available to help. Fast offerings provided for Gloria and José what they could not provide for themselves. Each child in the family dealt with the news in his or her own way, but all were impressed with their mother's strong faith. Gloria continued to smile, attend church, read her scriptures, and sing hymns.

Soon Gloria could no longer walk without help. Next she could not comb her hair or brush her teeth. This woman who had spent her life serving others now needed to be served. Her husband and family cared for her lovingly. Ward friends and missionaries helped.

When my mission ended and I was scheduled to leave Chile, I was invited to a farewell party hosted by Gloria and José and some friends in their ward. There were soft drinks, chips, and *roscas*—little fried donuts covered with powdered sugar. She knew I loved them. We had a pleasant time visiting, and Gloria was proud to tell me that the younger boys had decided to be baptized and were now preparing to go to the stake Young Men's camp. An older daughter, while not interested in baptism, was softening in her feelings about the Church. She no longer believed God was punishing her mother.

As a going-away gift, Gloria gave me a beautiful embroidered picture that she had made years earlier. The fact that her hands and arms would no longer allow her to create such a beautiful thing made the gift especially meaningful.

When the farewell party came to a close, it was difficult for me to control my emotions. My mission was ending. I would soon be returning to the United States, and it was likely that I would not see Gloria again in this life. I cried as I hugged her good-bye. Before I could say anything, she looked up at me and said, "Faith, President Wilcox, not fear."

I had been home less than a year when I learned of Gloria's passing. As I sent my condolences to the family, I knew she would be missed by all who knew and loved her. I also knew that Jesus had helped her every step of her difficult journey.

TO BE COMFORTED

Just as we are helped in times of sickness and disease, the Atonement also comforts us when we make mistakes. I will never forget being invited to speak along with Elder Robert E. Wells of the First Quorum of the Seventy at the women's facility at the Utah State Prison.

As I prepared my thoughts and outlined a short talk, I couldn't help but wonder what Elder Wells might say. What would this General Authority speak about at a prison? Would he call the inmates to repentance or express his love? Would he challenge them to reflect on the past or set goals for the future?

When the day finally arrived, I concluded my talk and then introduced Elder Wells to the women. Some of them were LDS and knew of him. For nonmembers he was a new face. They saw him only as a kindly grandfather who had come to share some advice. I don't think either members or nonmembers expected to receive the powerful and very personal testimony of the Savior that Elder Wells expressed.

"Jesus Christ died for our sins," he began, "but also for our mistakes." He then spoke about his first wife and their life together in South America, where he worked as an international banker. Because of the great distances they had to travel, they both had pilot's licenses and owned and operated their own planes.

On one occasion they flew from their home in Paraguay to Uruguay with some friends, where they attended the Saturday sessions of a Church conference. They planned to attend the Sunday meetings as well, but were advised of a bad weather report and decided to leave early, trying to return home ahead of the storm.

Everything was going as planned until they flew into some thick clouds and lost visual and radio contact with each other. Elder Wells flew on to the next airport where they had planned to refuel, only to be informed that his wife's plane had crashed and neither his wife nor the two passengers had survived. Securing a car, Elder Wells rushed to the crash site.

All in attendance at the prison were now listening intently. Elder Wells told them: "At the site whatever hope I had kept that the report had been wrong disappeared. I realized my wife was now taken from my side. Words will forever be inadequate in expressing the pain that swelled within me, consuming my emotions and numbing my senses. Profound tears of sorrow simply wouldn't stop flowing. To make matters worse, as my mind was attempting to deal with the devastating realization of my wife's passing, I found myself experiencing tremendous guilt for having somehow caused the crash."

Elder Wells explained how he berated himself for not having had the plane checked out better before they flew. He chastised himself for not giving his wife adequate instrument flying instructions. He felt he was guilty of neglect. Elder Wells continued: "That combined with the remorse and loss of two dear friends in addition to my beloved sweetheart became almost more than I could bear. Once the tears stopped, I simply lost my desire to continue on."

No one listening moved. Even the guards who were attending out of obligation were focused on Elder Wells. They realized that this man was sharing straight from his heart a story he rarely shared in public. The room was filled with respectful reverence.

Elder Wells went on: "The most difficult moment, of course, came when I had to tell our three children of their mother's death. They were seven, four, and one. I knelt down to be on their level and then, through unabashed tears, I told them of the accident. The two eldest ran and threw their arms around me—not seeking comfort, but to console me. Through the tears I was able to tell them that because of Jesus' Atonement their mother was still alive and we would once again be together as a family. These words brought with them a reassurance for each of us."

Then Elder Wells explained to the women at the prison that in the months and years that followed he was to discover more about the Atonement than he had ever understood before. Yes, it gave him the promise of his wife's resurrection and, if he lived worthily, their joyful reunion in the hereafter. However, he learned that the Atonement would also get him through the here and now. In fact, it was the only thing that could.

Elder Wells said: "Following my wife's funeral in the United States, and after returning to Paraguay with my three children, my mind went into a dark daze. I became a walking vegetable, able to function only on a minimal level. This I did for the sake of the children and for no other reason. Truly, I didn't see in color for the next year. Everything I saw was in black and white and had no beauty to it. I simply existed—nothing more.

"Then one evening, while on my knees in prayer, a miracle occurred. While praying and pleading to my Heavenly Father, I felt as though the Savior came to my side and spoke these words to my soul and to my ears: 'Robert, my atoning sacrifice paid for your sins *and your mistakes*. Your wife forgives you. Your friends forgive you. I will lift your burden. Serve me, serve your family and all will go well with you.'"

Now Elder Wells was in tears. I was dabbing my own eyes, as were most in the room.

Elder Wells concluded: "From that moment, the burden of guilt was amazingly lifted from me. I immediately understood the encompassing power of the Savior's Atonement, and I now had a testimony that it applied directly to me. While I had previously felt like I could have been swallowed up to destruction, I now realized that Christ had comforted me. Just as my mind and emotions had been at the darkest level, I now experienced light and joy like I had never before known. I was filled with a new desire to serve Christ, His Church, my family, and my employer. The guilt and despair had disappeared. As my mind assimilated what had transpired, I realized that I had been given an unearned gift—the Lord's unearned gift of grace. I didn't deserve it. I had done nothing to merit it, but he gave it to me nonetheless" (Wells, Family History).

Elder Wells finished and a closing prayer was offered, but no one wanted to leave. No one wanted to lose the Spirit that had been felt. One by one, the women came forward to greet Elder Wells. One by one, each whispered, "I needed to hear that," or, "You have given me hope," or, "I know how you felt." Each person realized to one degree or another that just as Jesus had comforted Elder Wells, He would also comfort and succor them "according to their infirmities" (Alma 7:12). Because Jesus gave His *all*, He can comfort us in *all* our sorrows and wipe away *all* our tears (see Revelation 7:17).

TO BE EMBRACED

I have interviewed many who feel as if the blessings of the Atonement are meant for others and not them—for General Authorities like Elder Wells and not for the rest of us. They don't feel like they qualify because their lives don't match what they consider to be the ideal:

One young man came home early from his mission.

Another is in his thirties and is yet unmarried.

A young woman never knew her father because her parents

divorced when she was little and he refused to maintain contact.

Yet another young woman went on a mission, married in the temple, and then found herself in an abusive relationship. She was divorced before her second anniversary.

A middle-aged woman was trying to earn a living at the same time she was raising her family as a single parent and didn't have enough hours in the day to do all expected of her.

Another sister felt she might as well be a single parent. Her husband was not a member and did nothing to support her in her efforts to bring up the children in the Church.

A middle-aged man was deeply troubled because his ex-wife left the Church when she divorced him and now the children, who remained with their mother, were being bombarded with anti-Mormon literature.

One mother was struggling to deal with her teenage daughter's suicide, although it had happened many years earlier.

A teenage boy was anxious for acceptance from other males and responded eagerly when a popular boy extended his friendship. He soon discovered sexual favors were expected to maintain the relationship. He tried to cover his guilt by convincing himself his new lifestyle was acceptable.

His father was wrestling with feelings of hurt, embarrassment, and guilt. His son now claimed to be homosexual and had left the Church and participated in demonstrations against it.

The list of struggles seems endless. Obviously, many people live their lives far from the situations they planned and hoped for when they were children. This gives us all the more reason to turn to the Savior, whose message is not just "Come unto me," but "Come as you are." He doesn't say, "Go get your act together and then come back when you fit the mold." He says, in essence, "Let's start right where you are, and go from there." Christ doesn't wait to offer blessings until our families all look like the happy groups whose pictures appear in the *Ensign* magazine or in TV commercials. He doesn't require us to fit any mold before He is willing to mold us.

Sister Chieko N. Okazaki has said: "[Christ is] not waiting for us to be perfect. Perfect people don't need a Savior. He came to save his people in their imperfections. He is the Lord of the living, and the living make mistakes. He's not embarrassed by us, angry at us, or shocked. He wants us in our brokenness, in our unhappiness, in our guilt and our grief" ("Lighten Up!" 5–6).

We've already learned that the Hebrew word that is translated into English as *Atonement* means "to cover." In Arabic or Aramaic, the verb meaning to atone is *kafat*, which means "to embrace." Not only can we be covered, helped, and comforted by the Savior, but we can be "encircled about eternally in the arms of his love" (2 Nephi 1:15). We can be "clasped in the arms of Jesus" (Mormon 5:11). In our day the Savior has said, "Be faithful and diligent in keeping the commandments of God, and I will encircle thee in the arms of my love" (D&C 6:20).

When young Joseph Smith faced experimental surgery on his leg with no anesthetic, he requested only to be held in the arms of his father (see Smith, *History of Joseph Smith by His*

Mother, 57). When my own daughter was just a toddler and developed a lung condition that made breathing difficult, the only way she would submit to the tests and endure treatment was in the arms of her daddy.

As long as we face discouragement, injustice, abuse, disease, and hurts of every kind—even when they come as a result of unintentional mistakes and accidents—we are not alone. Just as trials are a continuous part of life, so too is the Savior's Atonement continuous. Not only will Christ "abide" with us at eventide (see Luke 24:29), but because of the continuous power of the Atonement, He will be with us always (see Matthew 28:20). Jesus the Christ, the Messiah, the Anointed One will cover, help, and comfort. He will hold us in His strong embrace continuously.

Chapter 4

WHAT DOES IT MEAN TO BE REDEEMED?

Redemption is more than paying justice and bringing everyone back to God. It is mercifully giving us the opportunity of being comfortable there. Not only can we go home, we can also feel at home.

"Wouldn't it be easier to just wait till everyone dies and then do baptisms for the dead?" The question came from a frustrated missionary who had spent months in a difficult area trying to find new investigators. "Seriously, President," the young elder continued, "everyone is going to hear the gospel in the spirit world or in the Millennium. Everyone is going to have the chance to receive essential ordinances through temple work, so wouldn't it be better to just wait?" He opened his scriptures and went on with his argument. "Right in D&C 137 we are told that God won't hold people accountable for gospel laws they don't know, so wouldn't it be better to leave everyone in ignorance? Why are we beating our heads against a wall for nothing?"

"Oh, it's not for nothing," I assured him. "We're getting something."

"Besides sore heads?" he asked.

"Actually, *because* of our sore heads!"

Elder M. Russell Ballard wrote: "It isn't easy. No one ever said that it would be. The question for us to consider is, *Is it worth it?*" (*When Thou Art Converted*, 9; emphasis added). If we put off missionary work until later and leave people in ignorance, then not only do they go "out of this world into an eternal world, unprepared to meet their God" (Alma 48:23), but *we* miss out on the very experiences that can help us learn how to be more like the Savior.

I explained to the young missionary: "Baptism isn't the end. The temple isn't the end. The Second Coming isn't the end. Even the celestial kingdom isn't the end. They are all means to the *real* end, which is for each of us to become like God and Christ. We may be content to stay as we are and let others stay as they are, but Heavenly Father has a much different plan in mind."

C. S. Lewis wrote, "The command *Be ye perfect* is not idealistic gas. Nor is it a command to do the impossible. He is going to make us into creatures [who] can obey that command. He said (in the Bible) that we were 'gods' and He is going to make good His words" (*Mere Christianity*, 205).

To that end, can we be content to let people die and then do baptisms for the dead? Can we in good conscience let people remain ignorant of the Savior and the plan of redemption? Can we let them go about their lives content with so little when we could offer them so much more?

Obviously, millions will end up having to wait until they are in the spirit world to learn the truth, but in the meantime we must help as many as we can because what we offer makes a difference—the difference between merely existing and truly living, between stagnating and progressing.

The missionary was correct in saying that those who are ignorant of God's laws are not accountable and will have the opportunity to be saved in the end. But for now they have missed out—not just because they don't know about the

Atonement, but also because they have not yet felt its transforming power (see Romans 8:12). Jesus came not only to *save* us but also to *redeem* us. Most of my life I have thought the two terms were synonymous, since they are often used interchangeably. However, the second question in the temple recommend interview is, "Do you have a testimony of the Atonement of Christ and His role as *Savior* and *Redeemer?*" The words stress two separate aspects of Christ's mission, and having a testimony of both is essential.

If we view the Atonement as only a way to be resurrected after we die, what motivates us to live? If we view the Atonement as only a way to clean up after the messes we have made, what motivates us to avoid making messes? If we view the Atonement as only a comforting support when we deal with hurts and illnesses, why are we required to go through such trials in the first place? What motivates us to learn from those experiences rather than just endure them? In each case, the answers we seek are found only as we look beyond Christ's saving role to His redeeming role. As Latter-day Saints, we know not only what Jesus saved us *from* but also what He redeemed us *for*. We must be renewed, refined, and ultimately perfected in Him.

RENEWED IN CHRIST

Like many words, *redeemer* has multiple meanings. Customary definitions include one who buys or wins back; one who frees us from captivity or debt by the payment of ransom; one who returns or restores. However, in recent years I have come to appreciate an additional dictionary definition that adds significance to all others: A redeemer is one who changes us for the better, one who reforms and reshapes us. The Atonement of Jesus Christ buys us back, frees us from captivity, and returns us to God, but it also offers us much more than a grand reunion with our Heavenly Parents. Being recovered, rescued, reconciled, reunited, and reinstated would all ultimately be disappointing if we could not also be renewed.

If our whole goal were just to be in God's presence again, why would we have left it in the first place? We were already with God in the premortal existence, but were painfully aware that we were not like Him physically or spiritually. We wanted to be like our Heavenly Parents and knew it was going to take a lot more than just dressing up in their clothes as little children do. We needed to fill their shoes—not just clomp around in them. The Atonement reconciles us with God so that we can again be with Him and enjoy sweet association, but how sweet can that association be if we remain unchanged? The goal is not just being *with* God, but being *like* God.

It is common to hear people say, "God loves us and wants us back." This is only partially right. Christ's redemption doesn't just restore the status quo by putting us back where we were. It makes us better. Maybe you are old enough to remember the six-million-dollar man. (He would cost a lot more today!) At the beginning of the TV show a voice would say, "We can rebuild him. We can make him better than before." That is exactly what Jesus does for us. Redemption is more than paying justice and bringing everyone back to God. It is mercifully giving us the opportunity of being comfortable there. Not only can we go home, we can also feel at home.

"The Atonement is fundamentally a doctrine of human development, not a doctrine that simply erases black marks" (Hafen and Hafen, *Belonging Heart*, 79). "One who chooses Christ chooses to be changed. . . . The Atonement [is] the means whereby our hearts might be cleansed and our souls transformed and prepared to dwell with Christ and our Eternal Father. . . . The Atonement does more than fix the mistakes. It does more than balance the scales. It even does more than forgive our sins. It rehabilitates, regenerates, renews, and transforms human nature. Christ makes us better, worlds better, than we would have been had there been no Fall" (Millet, *Grace Works*, 53, 61, 95).

On the final page of the Book of Mormon, Moroni invites all to "come unto Christ" (Moroni 10:32). In the next verse, he then makes a distinction between Christ's saving role—"unto the remission of your sins" and His redeeming role—"that ye may become holy" (v. 33). Christ himself made a distinction between "having life" and having "it more abundantly" (John 10:10).

At Easter time we sing the hymn "He Is Risen." The text also speaks of Christ's saving role—His victory over death, his sacrifice to free us from sin—and His redeeming role. Notice the third verse:

He is risen! He is risen!
He hath opened heaven's gate.

We are free from sin's dark prison,
Risen to a holier state.
(Hymns, *no. 199; emphasis added)*

Elder Tad R. Callister said, "The Atonement was designed to do more than restore us to the 'starting line'—more than just wipe the slate clean. [Its] crowning purpose [is] to endow us with power so that we might overcome each of our weaknesses and acquire the divine traits that would make us like God" ("How Can I Lead a More Saintly Life?" 89).

The parable of the Good Samaritan can be viewed as an allegory of the Fall and redemption of mankind. A certain man (Adam) fell and was left for dead. Finally a Samaritan—He who was hated of men (Christ)—saved him (see Luke 10:25–35; Welch, "Good Samaritan," 41–47).

But the Samaritan didn't just bind the victim's wounds and restore him to the health he had enjoyed previously. He also took him to an inn and paid additional funds for his care. Based on this allegory, Christ's redemption does not stop with restoring us to life. That is only a step toward providing a better quality of life.

In Luke 17 we read of ten lepers who were cleansed by the Master. "And one of them, when he saw that he was healed, turned back, and with a loud voice glorified God, and fell down on his face at his feet, giving him thanks" (vv. 15–16). Jesus then asked the whereabouts of the other nine and was told that none of them had returned. Jesus spoke to the one, saying,

"Arise, go thy way: thy faith hath made thee whole" (v. 19). Ten lepers were healed that day, but only one was made whole.

A friend once told me, "Look, I'm a good person even though I don't go to church." I agreed, but gently reminded him that his goodness wasn't in question. He had already proven that in the premortal existence. This life is about becoming *better*. The English word *sacrifice* comes from two Latin words: *sacer*, meaning *sacred*, and *facere*, meaning *to make*. Christ's sacrifice is not just to make us free from the grasp of sin and death, but to make us sacred. The Atonement is not just to cleanse, but to complete; not just to comfort, but to compensate; not just to liberate, but to lift.

REFINED IN CHRIST

After a lesson about how Jesus had suffered for all of us, a young man once said to me, "I never asked Jesus to do that for me. If anyone has to suffer for my sins, I will do it for myself."

Clearly that prideful young man was ignorant of the amount and degree of suffering he was talking about. In D&C 19:18 the Lord says, "Which suffering caused myself, even God, the greatest of all, to tremble because of pain, and to bleed at every pore, and to suffer both body and spirit."

But along with not understanding the extent of the suffering, the boy was also ignorant of just what suffering can and cannot do. The scriptures make it clear that those who do not repent and accept Jesus' Atonement "must suffer even as [He did]" (D&C 19:16–17). So, will that cocky teenager be able to suffer for his own sins and then waltz into the celestial kingdom to live with God and his family eternally? Will he be beaten "with a few stripes, and at last . . . be saved in the kingdom of God" (2 Nephi 28:8)? No. The Book of Mormon makes it clear such an idea is false, vain, and foolish (see 2 Nephi 28:9).

Amulek taught, "He that exercises no faith unto repentance is exposed to the whole law of the demands of justice; therefore only unto him that has faith unto repentance is brought about the great and eternal plan of *redemption*" (Alma 34:16; emphasis added).

Although one can meet the demands of justice by suffering for his own sins, such suffering will not change him. Just as a criminal can pay his debt to justice by doing time in prison and walk out unreformed, suffering alone does not guarantee change. How many suffer through drug rehab programs and yet return to their old patterns when they leave? Even suffering death does not change a person's spirit (see Alma 34:34; Mormon 9:14). Lasting change, here and hereafter, comes only through Christ.

"The entrance requirements for celestial life are simply higher than merely satisfying the law of justice. For that reason, paying for our sins will not bear the same fruit as repenting of our sins. Justice is a law of balance and order and it must be satisfied, either through our payment or His. But if we decline the Savior's invitation to let Him carry our sins, and then satisfy justice by ourselves, we will not yet have experienced the complete rehabilitation that can occur through a combination of divine assistance and genuine repentance. Working together, those forces have the power permanently to change our hearts and our lives, preparing us for celestial life" (Hafen, *Broken Heart*, 7–8).

Like a sapling that bends and gets muddy during a storm, a person who is merely sorry to be soiled by sin will sin again in the next high wind. The susceptibility to repetition will continue until the sapling becomes a tree—a person so strengthened he no longer bends. Elder Dallin H. Oaks wrote, "The Savior does more than cleanse us from sin. He also gives us new strength. . . . To be admitted to His presence, we must be more than clean. We must also be changed" (*With Full Purpose of Heart*, 126–27).

We accept Christ not because it will save us some pain and suffering down the road, but because it is the only way we can become new creatures. We don't walk into the celestial kingdom simply because a debt is paid, whether it is paid by Jesus or—as difficult as it would be—by ourselves. The Atonement is not just about paying debts but about transforming debtors.

I have heard an acronym for *GRACE*: God's Riches At Christ's Expense. While this may be a clever and accurate definition, grace is also about preparing us to use those riches wisely and not squander them. God loves us and desires for us every privilege and blessing He can bestow, but we must acknowledge that privileges in the hands of the unprepared can often be curses rather than blessings.

PERFECTED IN CHRIST

Christ's Atonement overcomes the effects of the Fall, but it doesn't help us overcome bad habits unless we receive and apply it over time. "For what doth it profit a man if a gift is bestowed upon him, and he receive not the gift?" (D&C 88:33). Those who dwell with Christ are those who have come to be like Him through fulfilling what He asks. The justified must still be sanctified. The "new" must become "new and improved." Those who are declared "not guilty" must become worthy, even holy, and this doesn't happen automatically or quickly.

Christian friends ask me if I have been saved by grace. I always answer, "Yes—absolutely." Then I occasionally ask them if they have been *changed* by grace. We must never be so content to be saved by grace that we overlook the fact we must also be redeemed by grace.

We don't get into heaven on Jesus' coattails. Rather, He changes us until we fit His coat. Christ justifies by exchanging His goodness for our sin. He sanctifies by exchanging our worldly natures for a celestial nature. Justification alters our standing. Sanctification alters our state. Justification frees us from sin's penalty. Sanctification frees us from sin's tyranny (see Galatians 3:13; Philippians 3:8–9, D&C 76:69; see also MacArthur, *Faith Works*, 121). While justification is represented by clean hands, sanctification is represented by a pure heart that has been given to God (see Mosiah 4:2; Helaman 3:35).

If all we needed was an immortal body, God could have

given us one from the start. After all, He provided one for Jesus. But such a gift would have been like giving us a new car without teaching us how to drive. What is the point of looking like He looks or even having what He has if we are not living as He lives?

Many scriptures make it clear that we will be judged by our works, but those works are not fruitless attempts to pay justice. That bill has already been settled, if we'll accept it. Our works do not pay part or repay any of it. Rather, they help us resemble and serve the bill payer. To the extent that such a transformation takes place, we are indeed judged by our works.

Abinadi taught, "The Lord redeemeth none such that rebel against him and die in their sins; . . . that have known the commandments of God, and would not keep them" (Mosiah 15:26). These rebellious souls will all be resurrected and have the opportunity to repent, so in this sense they are saved. However, by choosing not to do what the Lord has asked of them, they missed out on the experiences that could have helped them improve. The Lord can't perfect them without their consent.

When I was younger I imagined the final judgment as a time when people would be begging Jesus to let them stay in His presence and He would have to say, "Sorry. You missed it by two points." Then the person would beg Jesus to reconsider. Now that I have more experience, I imagine the scene quite differently. Instead of an unrepentant person saying, "Let me stay. Let me stay," I think he or she will be saying, "Let me leave. Let me leave." Alma taught that people will be "their own judges" (Alma 41:7). The unrepentant will choose to leave Christ's presence because they will not be comfortable. I don't think people will have to be kicked out. Sadly, they will desire to leave on their own (see 1 Nephi 15:33; Alma 29: 4; Mormon 9:3). Scriptures teach that no unclean thing can enter into God's kingdom (see 3 Nephi 27:19), but no unchanged thing will even want to. Sinlessness is only one of God's attributes. There are many others that must also be obtained.

Elder Dallin H. Oaks wrote: "The final judgment is not just an evaluation of a sum total of good and evil acts—what we have *done*. It is an acknowledgment of the final effect of our acts and thoughts—what we have *become*. . . . A wealthy father . . . said to his child: 'All that I have I desire to give you—not only my wealth but also my position and standing among men. That which I *have* I can easily give you, but that which I *am* you must obtain for yourself. You will qualify for your inheritance by learning what I have learned and by living as I have lived'" (*With Full Purpose of Heart*, 38; emphasis in original).

INCOMPLETE ANALOGIES

I've heard our current mortal condition described with many examples. Some say we are in a hole. Others say we are in debt, lost, cut off, or standing on the far side of a wide chasm. Whatever the analogy, Jesus will not only save us by lifting us out of the hole. He will redeem us by lifting us to a much higher plane. He will not only save by paying the debt. He will redeem by paying us in addition. He will not only save by finding the lost, reinstating the alienated, or bridging the chasm. He will redeem by making us better.

I once saw the Fall and Atonement illustrated by a teacher who showed the class a plate and then proceeded to shatter it to demonstrate the effects of the Fall. The teacher ended by explaining how Jesus came to fix what was broken and produced a new plate. His object lesson grabbed everyone's attention, but the example assumes that we were perfect to start with—that before the Fall we were already in an ideal state—and such was not the case. The whole reason for the Creation was because our situation in the premortal existence was less than ideal. We wanted and needed better.

In the object lesson, mortality was represented by a shattered plate. While this seems a fair representation, it does not take into consideration the fact that we were joyful at the prospect of experiencing that shattered-plate world (see Job 38:4, 7). Just like Adam and Eve, we *chose* it because we knew it would be better for us in the long run. We knew that through the interaction of God's mercy and our obedience we could move beyond theory to experience.

We were not forced to come. We signed up because we knew the Atonement of Christ not only offered us a way back, it offered us a way to be better for having come. We would not just get a new plate, but a whole new set of beautiful china.

The Fall has also been compared to a little child being sent to his room because he misbehaved. After a time the child approached his parent and wanted to be friends again. Such an explanation overlooks the fact that, unlike the misbehaving child, we were "sent to our room" not because God was angry but because He was being our friend, our best friend. In the premortal existence we had done nothing wrong to merit being sent away. In our case the "room" wasn't a punishment, but a necessary next stage in our progress. The spirits who didn't get sent to this "room" to experience the privilege of mortality were the ones being punished. Because of the redemption offered by Christ, when we return we will not only still be friends with God, we will be better friends than ever because we will have so much more in common.

HIS IMAGE IN OUR COUNTENANCES

Jesus opened to us the possibility not just of returning to God's presence but of returning with His image in our countenance (see Alma 5:14). An elder in my mission once wrote: "I always wanted to see Christ. I always felt like that would be the ultimate, but if you think about it, everyone will see Him one day. Just seeing Him doesn't change a person. The ultimate is not seeing Him, but having Him see His countenance in us."

The first miracle of Jesus recorded in the scriptures is the changing of water into wine (see John 2:7–9). When I was a child, I couldn't get beyond the wine part. As a teenager, I became fascinated with whether or not it was Jesus' own wedding. As a missionary, I read *Jesus the Christ* and was touched by how Jesus called His mother *Woman* in respect and not rebuke (see Talmage, *Jesus the Christ*, 136). I was well into my adult years before I finally realized the main point of Christ's first miracle had little to do with wine, marriage, or titles. It had to do with change. Jesus was announcing in a dramatic way that He has the godly power to change things, even when it seems impossible.

When we fold our arms and exclaim defiantly, "It's just the way I am" or "I was born this way," we are denying the miracle of Christ—not just to save, but to redeem. If saving were all we needed, Satan's plan could have worked. He offered to get us back safely. It is the redeeming we would have missed—the possibility of having Christ's image would have been replaced with the surety of Satan's image. As Sheri Dew put it, "There is one thing the Lord and Lucifer have in common: *They both desire us to become as they are*" (*God Wants a Powerful People*, 104; emphasis in original). Satan wasn't willing to risk by trusting or helping us reach our potential. Christ was. He prayed that we might be one with Him as He is one with the Father (see John 17:11, 21–22). This heartfelt desire went way beyond a plea for unity. He was speaking about sameness. In Genesis we read, "God created man in his own image" (Genesis 1:27). Why would He start there if He didn't also intend to end there? An entirely new perspective awaits those who see "His own image" as the finish line and not just the starting block.

"Therefore, what manner of men ought ye to be?" asked the Savior. "Verily I say unto you, even as I am," He answered (3 Nephi 27:27; see also 2 Peter 3:11).

Sincere Latter-day Saints not only share this desire, but we know how it can become reality. We know what Jesus has asked of us in order to make such a transformation possible. From childhood we learn of faith in Christ, which includes repentance, and making and keeping covenants. We demonstrate faith by receiving essential ordinances from one having authority and we use the gift of the Holy Ghost to endure to the end.

"Only the restored gospel has the fulness of these truths! Yet the adversary is engaged in one of history's greatest cover-ups, trying to persuade people that this Church knows least—when in fact it knows most—about how our relationship with Christ makes true Christians of us" (Hafen, "The Atonement: All for All," 99).

It is one thing to see Christ standing at the door and hearing him knocking, and another to have the keys that open the door from the inside. And to those who open the door, Jesus said, "I will come in to him, and will sup with him, and he with me. To him that overcometh will I grant to sit with me in my throne, even as I also overcame, and am set down with my Father in his throne" (Revelation 3:20–21). Jesus chose to become like us so that we can choose to become like Him (see D&C 93:26; 1 Corinthians 2:16). This is what it means to be redeemed.

Saving requires an Atonement. Redeeming requires a continuous Atonement. Being born again requires an Atonement. Being reared to spiritual adulthood requires a continuous Atonement (see Ephesians 4:13). Knowledge of the Atonement is light. Realizing its continuous power in our lives is more light that grows "brighter and brighter until the perfect day" (D&C 50:24).

Chapter 5

ONE LONE BRANCH

Because Jesus was the firstborn spiritually and the only one foreordained by the Father, He was the only one authorized to atone for us. Because He had an immortal Father and a mortal mother, He was the only one capable of atoning for us. Because of His completely perfect life, He was the only one qualified to atone for us.

"I would have done it too," a young man told me after a lesson on how grateful we should be that Jesus suffered and died for us. The sincere boy said, "If I had been there I would have been willing to suffer for all my brothers and sisters. I would have been willing to die for them."

I was deeply touched by the young man's goodness and replied, "I think it is wonderful you feel such love and I don't doubt your willingness. Still, Jesus is unique because not only was He *willing*; He was *able*."

Because Jesus was the firstborn spiritually and the only one foreordained by the Father, He was the only one authorized to atone for us. Because He had an immortal Father and a mortal mother, He was the only one capable of atoning for us. Because of His completely perfect life, He was the only one qualified to atone for us.

Christ did what we couldn't do for ourselves or for each other. As much as a mother loves her son, she cannot atone for him. As much as a father loves a daughter, he cannot take her sins upon himself. As much as a husband loves his wife, he cannot save her or redeem her. Even those who enjoy the blessing of being sealed in the temple accept the realization that such a blessing is dependent on Jesus and our faithfulness to Him.

Because Jesus was mortal like us, we know He understands

us completely. Because He is immortal and perfect, we can trust Him completely. No wonder Truman G. Madsen wrote, "Is there any person in the universe who qualifies for such multiple roles? Only one" ("The Suffering Servant," 228).

The Book of Mormon prophet Amulek taught: "For it is expedient that there should be a great and last sacrifice; yea, not a sacrifice of man, neither of beast, neither of any manner of fowl; for it shall not be a human sacrifice; but it must be an infinite and eternal sacrifice. . . . And that great and last sacrifice will be the Son of God, yea, infinite and eternal" (Alma 34:10, 14).

Much earlier, Nephi had desired to know the things his father had seen and was asked, "Knowest thou the condescension of God?" (1 Nephi 11:13–16). The condescension of God is that although Jesus was foreordained to His atoning role, He was not forced. He did not have to come and descend below all things. God did not have to let Him. The need for an Atonement did not require Jesus to complete it or God to allow it. God and Jesus both condescended to help us because they knew they were our only hope. It wasn't just one possible way or even the best way—it was the only way. We know of at least one other who was willing to save us and said, "Send me" (Abraham 3:27). Thankfully, willingness was only part of the requirement of condescension. Jesus was the only one whose motives were pure. He was the only one great enough to become the least.

Nephi was told, "Behold, the virgin whom thou seest is the mother of the Son of God, after the manner of the flesh"

(1 Nephi 11:18). And Nephi said, "And I looked and beheld the virgin again, bearing a child in her arms. And the angel said unto me: Behold the Lamb of God, yea, even the son of the Eternal Father!" (1 Nephi 11:20–21). Jesus was God's Only Begotten in the flesh. His unique birth and mission were absolutely necessary because they constituted our only chance to avoid eternal destruction. Truly, there is no other name by which we can be saved.

AN ABSOLUTE NECESSITY

Some in the world see no need for saving, succoring, or redeeming. They believe such experiences can all happen without Jesus. Some non-Christian religions teach of an afterlife. They offer a measure of comfort and a sense of peace and perspective to people going through hard times. They promise better lives in the world to come if people conform to certain norms or standards, and all this without any mention of Jesus.

To me these teachings seem like the words of children who speak of a parent's money without ever considering how it was obtained. I recall when one of my own children heard me complain about never having enough money and said innocently, "Well, just go to the bank and get more."

In the same way, worshipers in many world religions enjoy a portion of the Spirit and parts of the truth. They make withdrawals—so to speak—by enjoying their religious perspectives without understanding who put that money in the bank, who did the work and made such benefits possible. Which of the founders of major world religions declared himself to be divine? Buddha did not. Muhammad did not. Nor did Lao-tzu, Confucius, Abraham, or Moses. Only one religious leader made such a claim and then backed it up by the way He lived, the things He taught, and the miracles He performed—Jesus Christ.

Did any of these leaders claim the willingness or power to be able to suffer and atone for the sins of the world? Did Buddha or Muhammad? Did the founders of Hinduism or Shintoism? No. The only one who claimed such a thing and actually completed it was Jesus Christ.

While all religions contain part of the truth, and many do much good, they are not all the same. Likewise, all religious leaders are not the same. While the blessings of the Atonement are and will be a reality for all, even those who are not yet aware of them, those priceless blessings didn't just happen by chance. They happened because of Jesus.

I recall attending a testimony meeting in a BYU ward where a young Asian woman stood to share her feelings. She was a recent convert from Buddhism and was in the United States for the first time. Her English was excellent, considering she had only recently begun studying it. So was her understanding of Christ, since it was also new. She stepped to the podium and began: "I hear you all speak of your love for the Savior, and I do not yet feel what you feel because I did not grow up like you. Where I grew up I never even knew I needed a Savior. I was raised loving Buddha, who taught if I behaved my next life would be better and if I misbehaved my next life would be worse. It all depended on me—my choices and my actions. And of course, I was sure my next life would be bad because I couldn't behave all the time."

The missionaries taught this young woman about the Fall and the Atonement. She continued, "I didn't see how Adam and Eve eating fruit had anything to do with me. I couldn't see how Jesus bleeding in a garden or on a cross had anything to do with me either."

Then she read the Book of Mormon and finally understood that had there been no Fall, she would never have been born in the first place. She had never formally learned of the effects of the Fall, but she knew about death and feared it. She did not necessarily label her poor choices as sins, but knew when she had done something wrong. Long before she knew no unclean thing could dwell with God, she knew that no unclean person could dwell with his or her own conscience. She knew about remorse for her own hurtful actions.

As she read the Book of Mormon, she realized that Jesus completed Buddha's teachings. Through Buddha she had learned there would be life after death. Now she knew it was Jesus who made that life possible. Through Buddha she had learned her actions had consequences, but now she knew it was Jesus who could alter the negative outcomes that follow negative choices. Jesus could provide a positive future despite a negative past. She continued, "Now I am beginning to understand why you say you love your Savior, and I am starting to feel something for Him too."

OUR ONLY CHANCE

My brother-in-law Bob Gunnell has always had a deep appreciation and love for the Savior, some of which can be traced back to a terrible accident that almost claimed his life when he was a young deacon. The family was living in Japan, where my father-in-law was stationed with the military. Dad and several other leaders had taken the Scouts camping in the Okutama Mountains.

The following is taken from a letter written on April 19, 1973, the day after the accident, by my father-in-law, Leroy Gunnell. He was writing to his two oldest children, who were attending Ricks College at the time:

"Mother and I are sitting in the intensive care ward of the Yokosuka Naval Hospital watching Bob as he lies unconscious. We nearly lost him yesterday. I hope when you receive this, you will join us in fasting and praying for him.

"What started out to be just a fun Scout outing ended far differently. It had been raining most of the weekend so the ground was wet and unstable. We took the boys on a hike which was about an hour and a half to the top. The view was excellent, and after we took a few pictures we started down a different trail than we used coming up. About a third of the way down, the trail became narrow and rocky, turning into a steep ravine. Bob grabbed a large rock to steady himself and it broke loose. I was just inches from reaching him, but couldn't. He fell 60 feet—about seven stories—and hit an incline. Then a falling rock hit him in the head, knocking him off the incline. As I heard the rock go crashing the rest of the way down the mountain, I was stunned and sick.

"I've never felt so helpless in my life. I could hardly shake myself back to reality. From what I'd seen and heard I just knew Bob was dead. I cried out to the Lord to help me get to him and in an almost mad frenzy I started down. I slipped and fell about 30 feet myself and finally managed to claw enough dirt, rocks, and roots to stop myself.

"When I looked in the direction Bob had fallen I could hardly believe my eyes. There he hung in midair draped like a towel over a single branch about the size of your arm that was growing out of the face of the cliff. He was unconscious and hung lifeless, perfectly folded on his stomach over that small limb—the only one in sight. I cried again to the Lord to help me get to him. There was still a 50-foot drop below him to nothing but rocks at the bottom.

"I started as quickly as I could down that rugged cliff. I crossed underneath Bob and started to climb up towards him. It was then the first motion came from him; one of his legs started twitching, followed a minute or so later by his left arm swinging ever so slightly. I was exhausted at this point yet I knew I had to get up to him before he fell again. When I finally got close to him by literally clinging to the side of the cliff, I was just sick at heart. He had several large gashes in his scalp and still appeared lifeless except for an occasional twitching movement of an arm or leg. I couldn't do a thing by myself. There wasn't even a place to stand except one slippery rock the width of my boot and a handhold on a rock next to Bob. I prayed as fervently as I ever have for the Lord to help me. Then I called and called to let the other leader, Brother Jensen, and the boys know where we were. After about 15 minutes they came into sight above me, but it looked like an impossible situation. They decided to hurry to the bottom and get a rope.

"By this time my leg muscles were beginning to quiver from the strain of standing in such an awkward position. And it made me suffer to see Bobby hanging there still dripping blood. I couldn't stand seeing him that way any longer so I reached out and took him by the seat of his pants and pulled him off the branch. With great effort I lifted him over into my lap and cradled him the best I could. I then laid my free hand on his head and gave him a blessing that he might live to reach the doctors. Brother Jensen returned about 30 minutes later with the rest of the Scouts and a rope. I know the Lord strengthened me during that time because I had been hanging onto the cliff at least 45 minutes by then.

"Even though help had arrived, our situation was still desperate. I couldn't see how in the world I was going to be able to tie a one-handed knot and then lower Bob to the other boys. Again, I felt the helpless, futile feeling I had earlier. When they finally got the rope to me, I somehow managed to wrap it around Bob's chest and tie a knot. Bob began to groan, but he was still totally unconscious. I'm not exactly sure how I managed it, but with brute force and a lot of supernatural strength given from the Lord, I finally lowered him down to the rest of the group.

"It was only then I became aware of my own injuries. It felt like I had cracked two or three ribs, and my right knee and left leg were very stiff and sore. My left shoulder ached. I realized then I could not have carried Bob another moment. I could hardly get myself down the cliff.

"Later an ambulance from Tachikawa Air Force Base arrived and took Bob and me to the hospital there. Mom, who had been notified of the accident, arrived at about the same time we did. It was determined by the doctors that Bob needed to be transferred to the Naval Hospital at Yokosuka because the best neurosurgeon in the Far East was located there. Bob, Mom, and I were flown by helicopter. The surgeon and a team of doctors and their assistants worked frantically through the night to save Bob's life. This morning he is still alive and stabilizing slightly, but he is in very critical condition and has not regained consciousness."

Needless to say, when they received this letter Bob's brother and sister felt great concern, as did grandparents, other relatives, and friends in the Church throughout Japan and in the United States. Many were worried and joined the Gunnell family in praying for Bob, who remained in a coma at the hospital.

After ten days, the doctor called my mother-in-law into his office and explained that, while he was pleased with Bob's physical recovery, he was not seeing the progress he had hoped for mentally. The doctor then prepared Mom for the worst, explaining that Bob could end up with no brain activity. Or he could come to, but spend the rest of his life with severe limitations. The doctor then suggested that the family ask for a military compassionate transfer to be near a mental hospital where Bob could be committed.

Mom was six months pregnant with their last child and facing this alone since Dad had returned home to Tokyo to care for the other children. Mom said, "It was one of the lowest points of my life. I felt emotionally devastated and very alone. I had spent most of my time sitting by Bob's bed. After the doctor spoke with me and presented such a bleak outlook for the future I was at a breaking point.

"I found a private place, locked the door, and sank down wearily on a couch. My head hung in total dejection between my knees. At that moment, I heard a man's voice. At first it startled me because I was sure I was alone and had locked the door. Then the gentle voice said distinctly and clearly, 'Let not your heart be troubled; neither let it be afraid.'"

Mom realized she was experiencing a very special manifestation of the Holy Spirit. The voice continued, "Peace I give unto you." An indescribable calm began to envelop her whole body. She knew Bob was going to be okay. She quickly called her husband and shared the sacred experience. They both agreed they had nothing to fear and looked forward with renewed hope and assurance.

The next morning Mom was sitting by Bob's bed, and about 10:00 he began to stir, stretched a bit, sat up, and looked around. He saw his mother, grinned at her, and in a surprised voice said, "Well, hi, Mom!" Ten days later they left the hospital and went home to Tokyo.

Bob still has some scars, mostly under his hair, but his

recovery has been complete. None of the concerns expressed by the doctor were realized. Prayers were heard. Priesthood blessings were honored. Support was received from Church members as well as many friends in the military. The doctors and nurses who cared so lovingly for Bob referred to him as their walking miracle.

Bob went on to serve a mission in the Philippines. Now he and his wife, Jeanne, have five children of their own, and their eldest recently finished his mission in Seattle. Whenever members of the family speak of the long-ago accident, it is always with great reverence. We realize the only thing that came between Bob and certain destruction those many years ago was one lone branch.

In the World Room of the Salt Lake Temple, the walls are covered with beautiful murals. On the front wall is a steep cliff with nothing between the top and the bottom except one lone branch. That mural has special meaning to Leroy and Mary Lois Gunnell, their son Bob, and our whole family.

Sometimes when I am in that room I look at the branch and recall the details of Dad's letter. What were the chances of Bob falling directly over that branch—the only one on the cliff? As quickly as his body was descending, he could have easily hit the branch, broken it off, and continued plummeting an additional six stories to the bottom. What were the chances of his landing on his stomach instead of his side or back? What were the chances his weight would be perfectly balanced over it? What were the chances the limb would hold for the entire time Bob needed it? It is not difficult for me to see God's hand in saving Bob.

When he fell from that cliff, the law of gravity made no exceptions for really nice guys. Bad things happen to good people. Bob's only hope was found in the form of one lone branch growing on the face of that sheer cliff—a branch sent from God strong enough to catch him, strong enough to hold him.

Hopefully, most of us will never go through such a traumatic experience. Yet, in a way, everyone already has. We were born into a fallen world. This mortal experience was for our good, but nonetheless full of peril. Jesus is the one lone branch that catches each of us. Amulek taught, "For it is expedient that an atonement should be made; for according to the great plan of the Eternal God there must be an atonement made or else all mankind must unavoidably perish; yea, all are hardened; yea, all are fallen and are lost, and must perish except it be through the atonement" (Alma 34:9).

Sheri Dew taught: "The Savior isn't our last chance; He is our only chance. Our only chance to overcome self-doubt and catch a vision of who we may become. Our only chance to repent and have our sins washed clean. Our only chance to purify our hearts, subdue our weaknesses, and avoid the adversary. Our only chance to obtain redemption and exaltation. Our only chance to find peace and happiness in this life and eternal life in the world to come" ("Our Only Chance," 66).

Only when we realize our complete dependence on Christ can we begin to feel the true gratitude He merits. Only as we realize the sure destruction awaiting us at the bottom of the cliff do we appreciate the one lone branch and the God who placed it there.

NO OTHER NAME

In his classes at Brigham Young University, Robert J. Matthews helped students understand how essential Christ is by posing some interesting questions: Was there an acceptable alternate plan, or alternate savior, if Jesus had not fulfilled His mission? Is the gospel the only way or just the quickest way? What would have happened if Jesus had not come? What if He had not been obedient to the end and not accomplished the Atonement? Was there a backup plan with an understudy waiting in the wings?

Brother Matthews has written: "Several years ago I discussed this topic with a group of teachers, and I noted that they were strongly of the opinion that if Jesus had failed, there would have been another way to accomplish salvation. They acknowledged that any other way probably would have been harder without Jesus, but, they said, man could have eventually saved himself without Jesus if Jesus had failed. Thus . . . these teachers were saying, in effect, that Jesus Christ was a convenience but not an ultimate necessity" (*A Bible! A Bible!* 265–66).

President Boyd K. Packer explained how erroneous such thinking is when he proclaimed, "I seldom use the word *absolute*. It seldom fits. I use it now—twice. Because of the Fall, the Atonement was *absolutely* essential for resurrection to proceed and overcome mortal death. The Atonement was *absolutely* essential as the means for men to cleanse themselves from sin and overcome the second death, which is the spiritual death, which is separation from our Father in Heaven" (*Let Not Your Heart Be Troubled*, 79; emphasis added).

"For there is none other name under heaven given among men, whereby we must be saved" (Acts 4:12). This marvelous teaching is so important that it is repeated in each of the standard works (see Moses 6:52; Mosiah 3:17; D&C 18:23) and in two cases was recorded before Jesus was even born. This was not doctrine that surfaced after Christ's life. It was doctrine from the beginning. Christ isn't a shortcut or an easier way. "He always has been the only Savior for all of mankind, and He always will be. There are no alternatives, no backup men, no substitute plans" (Matthews, *A Bible! A Bible!* 287).

Imagine when we were in the premortal existence learning of the plan of redemption and of the essential role of Christ's Atonement. "I think [the Devil] not only 'guaranteed' salvation without effort for everybody but also probably went around saying something like this: 'Now look, if you allow yourselves to be born into this world subject to the fall of Adam, subject to sin and to death, and if Jesus doesn't come through, then you have lost your salvation'" (Matthews, *A Bible! A Bible!* 288).

Can't you almost hear Satan saying, "Are you really going to put all your eggs in one basket? Are you really going to put all of your faith in one person? That would be like a boy falling off a vast cliff and then expecting to be saved by one branch."

Everyone knew Lucifer's alternative plan provided no

chance for eternal growth or progress. So perhaps one of the reasons he was successful in convincing so many to follow him was by instilling doubt in God's plan. I imagine Satan saying, "I know my plan doesn't offer you much, but at least it is a sure thing. God's plan offers much more, but it comes with a risk. Are you really willing to take that risk? Are you really willing to have faith in Christ when it is all just words and promises from someone who has never completed an Atonement before?"

There's no question that Satan sowed his seeds of doubt and fear from the beginning because he has never stopped. Right up to the last minute in the Garden of Gethsemane, he did all he could to thwart the Atonement. Jesus faced "the awesome power of the evil one" (Packer, "Atonement, Agency, Accountability," 69) and "all the horrors that Satan, 'the prince of this world' could inflict" (Talmage, *Jesus the Christ*, 568; see also John 14:30). No wonder Jesus was worried about his Apostles and pled with them to avoid temptation (see Matthew 26:40–44). He knew the tempter himself was there stirring up every doubt and fear imaginable (see JST, Mark 14:36–38).

The Atonement was a lot to ask of anyone, but we knew Jesus was not just anyone. We knew Jesus would not fail. We believed in Him and were certain our confidence was not misplaced. We knew He would encounter ridicule and rejection—even from members of his family (see John 7:5), but we knew He would never give up. We anticipated the terror and injustice of Gethsemane, but we knew Jesus would never say, "My will, not Thine, be done." We foresaw the torture and irony of

Calvary, but we knew Jesus would never proclaim, "Forget it. This is too much to ask."

Even when he cried out to God using the most intimate of titles, "*Abba* . . . all things are possible unto thee; take away this cup from me" (Mark 14:36), we knew God would not do this because Jesus' *Abba* is also our *Abba*. God could not take away Christ's bitter cup without causing bitter consequences for us. We knew God would stay the course because the cost of failure was too great. The prospect of losing us was totally unacceptable to Him, despite Jesus' plea. Even on Calvary, when Jesus was left all alone on the cross without the help of His Father, the Holy Spirit, or angels, we knew He would come through.

The very fact we were born on this earth is evidence we rejected Satan and had faith in Jesus Christ from the beginning. Those without bodies are the ones who doubted. So sure were the rest of us that, unlike Bob, who fell off the cliff by accident, we jumped. We took a flying leap. We knew we could have been shut out forever from the presence of the Eternal God and severed completely from the regenerating powers of the Spirit. We knew the risks and the possibility of destruction. Nevertheless, we still took the plunge because we also knew there would be one lone rescuing and redeeming branch. Unlike Bob, who may or may not have been better off for having fallen, we knew that in the end we surely would be. The knowledge of that singular lone branch gave us the confidence to choose to fall.

Like the branch portrayed in the mural in the Salt Lake Temple and the one that caught Bob, Jesus is there for us. "Jesus is *the* Being in the universe who holds the keys of unlimited power over sin, death, hell, sorrow, suffering, the bottomless pit, the devil, and captivity" (Skinner, *Garden Tomb*, 72; see also Revelation 1:18; 3:7; 9:1; 21:1–4). Jesus will not bend or break. His power to sustain will be available to each of us as often as we need it and for as long as it takes. One lone branch is more than enough because of the continuous power of the Atonement. Christ's strength is perfect, His grace is sufficient, and His love is eternal.

Chapter 6

"AFTER ALL WE CAN DO"

Christ's requirements are not so that we can make the best of the Atonement, but so that—on His generous terms—the Atonement can make the best of us.

"For we know that it is by grace that we are saved, after all we can do" (2 Nephi 25:23). This is one of the most widely quoted scriptures in the Church, yet it may also be one of the least understood. Until we fully comprehend it, the scripture can sometimes be a source of discouragement rather than hope.

The meaning of a sentence can change depending on which word is emphasized. For example, if we say, "THAT lady said it," the meaning is different from stating, "that LADY said it," "That lady SAID it," or "That lady said IT." In the same way, as we vary the emphasis on the words found in 2 Nephi 25:23, we see the verse in a new light.

AFTER ALL WE CAN DO

For a long time I believed the word *after* in this verse was time related. I believed I had to do all I possibly could and then grace would kick in—as if it were a finishing touch to all I had to first accomplish alone. Then I thought of Paul and Alma the Younger, who did nothing first—or even at all—and yet received great spiritual blessings. I reflected on the many manifestations of grace in my own life that I had received long before I did "my part."

Donald P. Mangum and Brenton G. Yorgason point out that if we see the verse in the context of the chapters surrounding it, we see "that Nephi simply wasn't focusing on the central importance of our works, or 'doing all we can do' first. In fact, much to the contrary, he was delivering a message concerning the central importance of the mission of the Messiah . . . [and] the magnitude of the great gifts that come from him" (*Amazing Grace*, 58).

For example, in the very next chapter (2 Nephi 26:25) Nephi extends the invitation to "Come . . . buy milk and honey, without money and without price." No time condition is mentioned. Perhaps this is why the word *after* could also be read as *in spite of*. We are saved by grace in spite of all we can do (see *Amazing Grace*, 61).

Stephen E. Robinson wrote, "I understand the preposition 'after' in 2 Nephi 25:23 to be a preposition of separation rather than a preposition of time. It denotes logical separateness rather than temporal sequence. We are saved by grace 'apart from all we can do,' or 'all we can do notwithstanding,' or even 'regardless of all we can do.' Another acceptable paraphrase of the sense of the verse might read, 'We are still saved by grace, after all is said and done'" (*Believing Christ*, 91).

Christ's power is not an emergency generator that turns on once our supply is exhausted. It is not a booster engine once we run out of steam. Rather, it is our constant energy source. If we think of Christ only making up the difference *after* we do our part, we are failing to keep the promise we make each Sunday to remember Him *always*. Elder Bruce C. Hafen confirmed,

"The Savior's gift of grace to us is not necessarily limited in time to 'after' all we can do. We may receive his grace before, during, and after the time when we expend our own efforts" (*Broken Heart*, 155).

Such words provide comfort for the man who once wrote me the following: "I am told often that Christ will come to me only after I've jumped through an endless number of hoops. If I just do this or that or be really good then I too can feel Christ's love. The problem is that I need Him here and now and not at some future date. I could really use a shot of Christ's love and grace today."

If we believe we have to be completely worthy before we approach God, we will never be able to. Those who feel like failures don't usually fight for a front-row seat at heaven's throne. Instead we distance ourselves even farther from the source of worthiness we seek. Maybe we do this out of embarrassment, lack of confidence, low self-esteem, or for many other motives. Whatever the reason, we are all too quickly caught in a never-ending cycle of procrastinated change and postponed happiness.

Consider these words from a discouraged returned missionary: "I just read a book about changing my life, and instead of feeling motivated, I feel depressed. I'm a living paradox. I want to change and live right so I can be forgiven, but I need to be forgiven so I can live right. I want to do my part so I can receive the Savior's grace, but I need that grace to do my part, and it just keeps going like that. It is the same with girls. I want to date good Mormon girls, but I don't feel like I am good enough."

We can all appreciate this young man's struggles, but when he realizes he doesn't have to wait for grace, that it isn't up to him to do all he can *first*, then he will recognize that Christ will help him all the time. Suddenly, there is no paradox (and no excuse). The light isn't just at the end of the tunnel, it is all around him. He can quit blaming God for his lack of progress, quit waiting to ask out the Mormon girls, and be the success story someone can write a book about!

AFTER *ALL* WE CAN DO

The word *all* becomes tricky when most of us never feel we can do *all* that is possible. I remember reading the biography of President Spencer W. Kimball when I was quite young. I was amazed by how much this prophet could accomplish in twenty-four hours. He awoke early, went to bed late, and filled each day to the maximum. He typed letters and wrote thank-you notes as he rode in cars. He scheduled interviews between meetings and often left meetings to take plates of food to security guards.

Whenever I have an especially busy schedule, I call it a President Kimball day. Then I become discouraged when I can't keep up a similar pace all the time. Well-meaning friends say, "Just do your best," but I rarely hear those words as comforting advice. Instead, they seem like a challenge to push myself even harder.

My children tease me about always being late. They even bought me a license-plate holder that reads, "Always late, but worth the wait." Like many people, it's not that I want to be late. It's just there is always one more thing that needs to be done or one more person who desires to talk. My wife and I stay after church so often visiting with people that our exasperated children have decided we must have been foreordained to be the last ones out of every meeting.

Once, after helping to clean up after a ward activity, I arrived home late and exhausted. I collapsed on the family room couch and said, "I'm beat. I don't think I could do one more thing."

My daughter teased, "What? Dad stopping already? Surely there is still time to bake bread for the widows." The sad thing is I actually checked my watch to see if I could squeeze it in!

It has been said that doing "all we can do" is like paying tithing. Both the person who makes a million dollars and one who makes much less pay the same ten percent. Although the amounts are different, it's a full tithing for each of us. Nonetheless, the idea doesn't stop me from feeling that if I earned more I could pay more. I know this probably sounds pretty strange to some people. It is, however, how I have sometimes felt and stands as one example of the many times when I don't feel my "all" is enough.

One speaker in Church directs, "You can't do everything. Don't run faster than you have strength" (see D&C 10:4). The next says, "Push yourself. You can always do more." One person advises, "Don't worry about what you can't do" at the same time someone else says, "You can do anything you put your mind to." In one hymn we sing, "I need thee every hour," and in another we sing, "We will work out our salvation" (*Hymns*, no. 98, 254).

In this world of mixed messages, I never can seem to escape the nagging thought, "If only I were better organized or if only I tried harder." Satan tempted Christ with the word *if* (see Matthew 4:3–11). He often comes to me with the words *if only*.

"Don't worry about if you have done enough," advises one well-meaning friend. "Rather, ask if what you have done is acceptable to God." The problem with such advice is that I can't figure out how anything less than my all could ever be acceptable. I am told the companionship of the Spirit will be my assurance when I've done my part. However, if I start beating myself up for not being a better home teacher or helping more with family history, then I can drive the Spirit away pretty quickly.

In those anxious moments, the greatest comfort I have found is in knowing *any* effort is pleasing to God even if He and I both know it's not my all or my best. It may be far from an acceptable offering, but God accepts it nonetheless because ultimately He is more concerned with the offerer than the offering. Elder Gerald N. Lund wrote: "Remember that one of Satan's strategies, especially with good people, is to whisper in their ears: 'If you are not perfect, you are failing.' This is one of his most effective deceptions. . . . We should recognize that God is pleased with every effort we make—no matter how faltering—to better ourselves" ("Are We Expected to Achieve Perfection in This Life?" 207).

Often I am the first to acknowledge that my efforts are mediocre at best. But instead of feeling bad about not offering more, I recognize it's a step in the right direction. I remind myself that the word *mediocre* is from the Latin word *mediocris*, which means halfway up the mountain. It doesn't describe how far I can go. It just indicates how far I have come. If I am halfway up the mountain and on my way to the top, it is better than being at the bottom and refusing to try. No matter where I am on the mountain, the motivation to climb higher is found not in trying to impress God and Christ with my sacrifices, but in letting their sacrifices be more deeply impressed upon me.

AFTER ALL WE *CAN* DO

What can any of us do without God? The older we get, the less we have to be reminded of the "greatness of God" and our own "nothingness" (Mosiah 4:11). Our dependence on Christ's enabling power becomes more apparent with each passing day.

After Moses' amazing encounter with God, the prophet declared, "Now, for this cause I know that man is nothing, which thing I never had supposed" (Moses 1:10). "God . . . withdrew His presence from Moses so that Moses could come to understand that his very life-energy and strength came from God, and that without God he would be nothing. Moses fell to the earth, and for the space of many hours he experienced the contrast of being without God's sustenance. . . . The term nothing, in this context, does not mean worthless or valueless, for Moses' infinite worth and value had already been magnificently communicated to him in ways which far transcended anything he had ever experienced or visualized. *Nothing* means powerless" (Covey, *Divine Center*, 172–73; emphasis added).

"I can do all things through Christ which strengtheneth me" said Paul (Philippians 4:13). The Book of Mormon testifies that the Lord is our every breath and heartbeat (see Mosiah 2:21). Isaiah wrote, "But now, O Lord, thou art our father; we are the clay, and thou our potter" (Isaiah 64:8). With such scriptures in mind, we no longer need to read the words *after all we can do* as a statement. Along with Robert L. Millet, we can rearrange them into a question: "After all, what can we do?" (*Grace Works*,135).

About a year after the death of her husband, a widow was asked, "When did you feel like Christ stepped in and made your burden bearable?"

She responded, "Was there ever a time when He wasn't shouldering the whole load? There were never two sets of footprints in my sand—only one, and it was always His."

Who is bold enough to assume there has ever been a time, however short, when we were not being sustained by Christ? We may not have been aware of His grace, but it was there. To boast otherwise would be like a jockey claiming he could win a race without his horse.

When I was younger I sometimes told the youth, "Give Christ an inch and he'll take you a mile." It seemed a clever twist on an old phrase. However, now I realize that if we will simply turn to Him, He will take us both the inch and the mile.

Many of us have heard an analogy in Sunday lessons that goes something like this:

There is a man in a hot desert who sees a fountain at the top of a hill. With great effort, he climbs the hill and receives the life-giving water. What saved him? Was it the climb (his works) or the water (grace)? The answer, of course, is that they are both essential (see Pearson, *Know Your Religion*, 92–93).

While effective in teaching the necessity of both grace and works, the analogy doesn't fairly illustrate the interaction between the two or the extent to which the Savior goes to enable us. The water may be at the top of the hill, but that's not where Christ is. He comes down to the bottom and brings the water to us. That's how we can make the climb to the top—which He still requires because He knows it will strengthen us and be for our best good. Christ is not waiting at the finish line; He is finishing our faith (see Hebrews 12:1–2). Grace is not the prize at the end of the climb. It is the enabling power throughout (see "Grace," *Bible Dictionary*, 697).

We read in scripture of Moses, Enoch, Gideon, and Jonah—all great men who did not initially believe they were capable of doing what God called them to do. However, as we know, with the Lord's help they succeeded (see Exodus 4:10; Moses 6:31; Judges 6:15; Jonah 1–3). They learned, "For it is God which worketh in you" (Philippians 2:13). Isaiah promised, "Hast thou not known? hast thou not heard, that the everlasting God . . . giveth power to the faint; and to them that have no might he increaseth strength?" (Isaiah 40:28–29).

This earth life is rightly described as a school, but we have a Father and an older brother who not only paid the tuition but also help us with our homework! I no longer say, "The Lord helps those who help themselves," but instead, "The Lord helps us *to* help ourselves."

AFTER ALL WE CAN *DO*

Some people see a long checklist that must be completed before we get to heaven. In reality, our willingness to plod along here on earth doesn't earn us points in heaven, but helps us become heavenly. We are not called human *doings;* we are human *beings*. Doing is only a means to being.

Scriptures make it clear that our works are a significant factor in where we end up. However, this is not because of what our works earn us, but because of how they shape us. Andrew C. Skinner wrote, "Our condition in eternity will not be determined by what happened *to* us but rather what will happen *in* us as a result of the Savior's atonement" (*Garden Tomb*, 56; emphasis in original). In reality, we are not human doings or human beings. We are humans *becoming* (see David A. Bednar, "Becoming a Missionary," 44–47; Dallin H. Oaks, "Challenge to Become," 32–34). Christ said, "Follow me, and I will make you fishers of men" (Matthew 4:19), but let's occasionally leave off a few words and hear Him saying, "Follow me, and I will make you."

When Naomi W. Randall wrote the words to "I Am a Child of God" (*Hymns*, no. 301), she wrote, "Teach me all that I must know." President Spencer W. Kimball suggested the lyric be changed to "Teach me all that I must do" because knowledge is of little worth unless it is acted upon. Perhaps one day we will all sing, "Teach me all that I must be." In the final analysis, it is not what we know or even what we do that will matter, if by then we have not become the kind of people who can "live with Him someday" (see Black, *Finding Christ*, 49–50).

I once spoke with a sister missionary about her feelings of inadequacy. Through her tears she said, "I'll never be able to make the celestial kingdom. Perhaps I should just shoot for a lower kingdom and make my life a lot less complicated."

Does life really get less complicated if we lower our goals and settle for less? I suggested that a better solution would be learning where to turn for help. I told this faithful sister, "Picture yourself speaking to one of your investigators. What would you tell her if she felt like you do?"

The sister missionary took a deep breath and responded, "I would tell her to not give up. God is not quite finished with her yet."

Saints all around the world sing a favorite hymn, "Come, Come, Ye Saints" (*Hymns*, no. 30), in which the question is asked, "Why should we think to earn a great reward if we now shun the fight?" Is that really what we are doing—*earning* a great reward? The word *earn* doesn't appear even once in the Doctrine and Covenants. As we face the fight rather than shunning it, God transforms us. The final destination may be "far away in the west," but development is found all along the trail. The "great reward" is not just something we will receive, but what we become through the grace of Jesus Christ.

As a recent *Ensign* article explained: "Do we believe that His grace is necessary to our salvation? Absolutely. Without the grace of Jesus Christ, no one could be saved or receive eternal blessings. Through His grace, all will be resurrected and all who believe and follow Him may have eternal life. Moreover, through His grace, our sacred relationships with spouses and family can continue through eternity. These eternal blessings are His gifts to us; there is nothing we could do of ourselves alone that would merit or earn them. Nevertheless, the scriptures make it clear that we receive the full blessings of His grace through our faith and obedience to His teachings (Ephesians 2:8–10; James 2:17, 24)" ("We Believe," 55–56). What are the "full blessings" of His grace if not fulfilling the measure of our creation by becoming more like God and Jesus?

AFTER ALL *WE* CAN DO

After examining all other options with our scriptural phrase, we are left with just one. It is to emphasize the word *we*—not *we* as in you and me, but *we* as in each of us with Jesus. It is this relationship which is the key to understanding 2 Nephi 25:23. It is by grace that we (you and I) are saved, after all we (Christ and each of us) can do together.

In the Doctrine and Covenants we read a similar scripture: "Let us cheerfully do all things that lie in our power; and then may we stand still . . . to see the salvation of God" (D&C 123:17). At first that seems like a restatement of the scripture in 2 Nephi, but consider who gave the revelation. Perhaps the words *us*, *our*, and *we* are not referring to you and me, but to Christ and us. C. S. Lewis put it this way, "We are now trying to understand, and to separate into water-tight compartments, what exactly God does and what man does when God and man are working together" (*Mere Christianity*, 149).

Scriptures speak of Christ's relationship with the Church as a marriage (Ephesians 5:22–23). However, Latter-day Saints know there is a difference between a marriage and a sealing. Christ doesn't just intend to "marry" us, but to seal us His (see Mosiah 5:15). One of Jesus' names, Emmanuel, means *God with us* (see Matthew 1:23–25). Is there a better definition of grace than this?

In the greatest of all companionships, one partner's offering is not stacked on top of the other's as if we must meet some minimum height requirement demanded by justice. It is not about height, but growth. We don't reach heaven by seeing Jesus' grace supplementing our works or our works supplementing His grace (see 2 Nephi 31:19; Moroni 6:4). Heaven is not reached by supplementing, but by covenanting; not by defining a ratio, but by building a relationship; not by negotiation, but by cooperation and union. Instead of seeing two *parts*, we might do well to see two *hearts* working in conjunction and being conformed to the same image (see Romans 8:29; Galatians 4:19).

In the final question of the temple recommend interview each person is asked to make an evaluation as to his or her personal worthiness. The question gives us all a chance to pause and thoughtfully consider. One sister I interviewed while serving as a member of her stake presidency did not pause in the slightest. She confidently said, "Alone I am not worthy, despite all the questions I just answered correctly, but don't worry,

President. I'm not alone. I am standing hand in hand with the Savior, and together *we* are worthy."

Robert L. Millet wrote: "In a word, we are incomplete, or partial, whereas Christ is whole, or complete. As I come unto Christ by covenant, we (Christ and I) are complete. I am unfinished; Christ is finished. Through relying alone upon the merits of 'the author and finisher of [my] faith' (Hebrews 12:2; compare Moroni 6:4), I become finished, or fully formed. I am deeply imperfect; Christ is perfect. Together we are perfect. Those who come unto Christ become perfect *in him* (Moroni 10:32)" (*Grace Works*, 130; emphasis in original).

I once spoke with a college student who sought a better understanding of the Atonement. "I know," she said, "I have to do my part and then Christ does the rest, but the problem is that I can't even do my part." She then went on to list the many things she should be doing, but wasn't. She also spoke of the anger and jealousy she shouldn't be feeling, but was. Continuing, she said, "I know Christ can fill the gap between my best efforts and perfection, but who fills the gap between the way I am and my best efforts?"

I pulled out a paper and drew two dots on it—one at the bottom and the other at the top. "Here is God," I said, labeling the top dot. "And here we are," I said, indicating the bottom dot. How much of this distance does Jesus fill and how much is our part?" She started to mark a line at the halfway point and then thought better and marked a line much lower. I said, "Wrong."

"Is the line higher?" she asked.

"No," I responded. "The truth is, there is no line. Christ has already filled the whole distance."

"Right! Like I don't have to do anything?"

"Oh, no. You have plenty to do, but it is not to fill this gap. Jesus filled the gap that stands between us and God. It is done. We are all going to go back to God's presence. Now the question is how long we hope to stay there. That is what is determined by our obedience to Jesus."

Christ asks us to show faith in Him, repent, make and keep covenants, receive the Holy Ghost, and endure to the end. By complying we are not paying the demands of justice—not even the smallest part. Instead we are appreciating what Jesus did and using it to live the life of a disciple and follow a pattern set by Christ himself—what Joseph Smith called "the life of the righteous" (*History of the Church*, 2:229). Justice requires perfection or a punishment when perfection is not achieved. Jesus, who paid justice (see 2 Nephi 2:7), can now forgive what justice never could. By releasing us from the requirements of justice, He is now able to make a whole new arrangement with us (see 3 Nephi 28:35).

"So what's the difference?" the girl asked. "Whether our efforts are required by justice or by Jesus, they are still required."

"True, but they are required for different purposes, and that makes all the difference. Fulfilling Christ's requirements is like paying a mortgage instead of rent, investing instead of paying off debts, really getting someplace instead of walking on a treadmill, ultimate perfection instead of forever coming up short."

"But I already told you, I can't be perfect."

"You don't have to be, because justice is no longer in charge. Jesus is, and He only asks that you be willing to be perfected."

CHRIST'S GENEROUS TERMS

Christ's arrangement with us is similar to a mom providing music lessons for her child. Mom, who pays the piano teacher, can require her child to practice. By so doing she is not attempting to recover the cost of the lessons, but to help the child take full advantage of this opportunity to live on a higher level. Her joy is not found in getting her investment back but in seeing it used. If the child, in his immaturity, sees Mom's expectation to practice as unnecessary or overly burdensome, it is because he doesn't yet share her perspective. When Christ's expectations of faith, repentance, covenants, the gift of the Holy Ghost, and endurance feel trying to us, perhaps it is because, as C. S. Lewis put it, "we have not yet had the slightest notion of the tremendous thing He means to make of us" (*Mere Christianity*, 205). We are helped in this line-upon-line discovery when we focus less on *what* Jesus asks and more on *why* He asks it.

Elder Bruce C. Hafen wrote, "The great Mediator asks for our repentance NOT because we must 'repay' him in exchange for his paying our debt to justice, but because repentance initiates a developmental process that, with the Savior's help, leads us along the path to a saintly character" (*Broken Heart*, 149).

Similarly, Elder Dallin H. Oaks has taught, "The repenting sinner must suffer for his sins, but this suffering has a different purpose than punishment or payment. Its purpose is *change*"

(*Lord's Way*, 223; emphasis in original). Without the faith and repentance required by Christ there would be no redemption because there would be no *desire* for improvement. Without the covenants and the gift of the Holy Ghost there would be no *means* for improvement. And without the endurance required by Christ there would be no *internalization* of the improvement over time. Just as Jesus obeyed the will of the Father, we must now obey the will of Jesus. Christ's requirements are not so that we can make the best of the Atonement, but so that—on His generous terms—the Atonement can make the best of us.

Elder Melvin J. Ballard explained the Atonement by comparing it to one man paying off another man's home. The new homeowner says, "Now I know this was your home, and I know you love it. I know you are very sorry to lose it. . . . It is [now] mine, but I propose to give it back to you on certain conditions. . . . It is possible for you to fulfill them. [And then] I will not only give it back to you as it was, but I will glorify it also. I will make it more splendid and more wonderful than ever, and I will give it to you forever and ever" (Hinckley, *Sermons and Missionary Services*, 169).

Elder Ballard's example took on added meaning in my life when I realized Jesus, the new homeowner who paid the debt, intends to improve not just the home but also the previous homeowner. "Certain conditions" are required in an effort to remodel a person along with a home. We are the ones Christ intends to make "more splendid and more wonderful than before . . . forever and ever."

Such a continuous work requires continuous enabling

power. It requires more grace than can neatly be diagrammed, graphed, charted on whiteboards, or found in a concise listing of contractual responsibilities. Such power is found by going beyond defining parts and instead forging a relationship with God and Christ that is greater than the sum of the parts. When we do finally pass through the veil that separates us and the celestial kingdom, it will not be as individuals who have done our parts. It will be holding hands with Jesus. On that sacred day there will be no *He* and *I*—only *we*.

Chapter 7

WHO MADE GOD THE ENEMY?

God and Christ have been victorious and Satan and his followers have been thwarted at each essential turning point except one—the turning point in our individual lives. Satan cannot undo the Creation, the Fall, the Atonement, or the Restoration. He cannot pull them down, so instead he tries to pull us down.

"Jesus ransomed us. He paid our debt," testified one elder, just as he had many times in many lessons with many investigators.

Suddenly this particular investigator surprised him by blurting, "That's about the biggest bunch of capitalistic baloney I've ever heard!"

The missionary and his companion sat in stunned silence. They had never encountered such a response before.

The investigator continued, "All this talk of debt and ransom sounds totally North American to me. Everything has a price tag. Everything has to cost money. Even salvation has to be paid for. The whole story of Jesus suffering is nothing more than a capitalistic plot."

The elders tried to speak, but before they could get in a word, the man plowed ahead, saying, "If God *does* exist, He must be pretty mean and heartless to require someone's death as the price of salvation—especially someone who wasn't even guilty. And if Jesus *is* God's son, God must be a pretty lousy father to make Him do that."

Needless to say, the missionaries left the lesson feeling discouraged and confused. Over the next few days they discussed the man's views between themselves. Could it be true that the story of mankind being in debt to God was simply invented and perpetuated by Christian churches in order to subject people to their norms and get gain? There would be no better way to insure substantial financial donations than to constantly be telling people how in debt they were.

And why *did* God require the sacrifice of Jesus? How does that pay any debt? Jesus prayed submissively, "Not my will, but thine" (Luke 22:42), but why was His inexplicable suffering and horrible death God's will? How is anyone supposed to love a God who wills that?

God is the one who *placed* Adam and Eve in the Garden of Eden, and then *allowed* Satan to tempt them, so doesn't that make God partly responsible for the Fall? Why did He blame Adam and Eve? And if someone had to suffer to make things right again, why did He send Jesus? Why didn't God just do it Himself?

By the time interviews with the mission president rolled around, these two elders had quite a list of questions they wanted to discuss. After listening to the whole experience, I said, "Now you know why I'm glad I'm a Mormon! Questions like these have baffled many religious people and their leaders for years, but they don't baffle us."

The restoration of the gospel was not just another retelling of the same old stories. It was a restoration of the complete truth that surrounds the stories with purpose and perspective.

The story of the Creation wasn't new. However, the Restoration added the knowledge of the premortal existence. Now people could understand why God needed to create an earth for His children in the first place.

The story of the Fall wasn't new, but the Restoration added the knowledge of a mortal probation. Now people could understand why Adam and Eve's choice was wise and prudent rather than selfish and sinful—and why the consequences, though difficult, were desirable. Now people could understand that God wasn't blaming or punishing them, but ultimately helping them.

The story of the Atonement wasn't new, but the Restoration added the knowledge of eternal laws and the spirit world. Now people could understand the reason for the rules and how opportunities to make correct choices are offered many times before any final judgment occurs.

I said to the concerned missionaries, "As Latter-day Saints we are unique in our understanding that there are certain things that even God cannot do. He cannot annihilate us. He cannot take away our freedom, and He cannot break laws such as justice and mercy that coexist with him."

Alma taught, "The work of justice could not be destroyed; if so, God would cease to be God" (Alma 42:13). God is God not just because He is the law giver (see D&C 88:42), but because He is the law *obeyer*.

"So God is not the enemy," one of the elders concluded. "He is bound by the law of justice. So the law of justice is the enemy."

His companion said, "But if justice is the enemy, then God is a weakling. What is justice that it can control God? How can He be all powerful if He can't change the law, or stand up to it, or at least make a few exceptions? Even earthly laws allow for executive pardons."

In reply I said, "We know God is all powerful (see Alma 7:8; 26:35), so I assume He could somehow remove the law, but not without inviting chaos, and that would be unacceptable to Him. Along with being all powerful, God is all knowing (see Mormon 8:17; D&C 88:41). He realizes that conforming to the law is the only way He can truly preserve freedom, which is absolutely essential for our progress and happiness."

I once learned from an astute teacher, Terryl L. Givens, that one of the greatest contributions of the Book of Mormon is the way it clarifies that justice is not equivalent with God himself. Rather, it is an essential ingredient in the agency God gives us. When we explain the Atonement as being necessary only as a means of satisfying the demands of an inflexible principle called justice, we simply accentuate one of God's attributes over all others and overlook God's motive. Similarly, if God's mercy or compassion were allowed to completely override all other attributes, it would be a curse rather than a blessing, for it would limit our freedom to choose for ourselves (see Alma 41–42). Only the Book of Mormon presents both justice and mercy within the larger perspective of moral agency. Freedom can't exist unless we have the ability to act independently. Such action requires knowledge and the presence of real alternatives complete with real consequences (see 2 Nephi 2). Brother Givens explains: "The rationale behind such a moral order is not an omnipotent, impersonal, and cruelly inflexible absolute called justice, but rather the protection of a necessary framework for human agency. . . . No escape from the consequences of law is possible without destroying the entire moral order of the universe" (*By the Hand of Mormon*, 207).

If God determined to waive the requirements of the law and let us in some back door to heaven, then Jesus' suffering and death were needless. Such is not the case. Scriptures say that no unclean thing can dwell with God (see 1 Nephi 10:21), but no *unfree* thing can dwell with Him either. In Alma 61:15 we read of "the Spirit of God, which is also the spirit of freedom." God willingly conformed to the law, and Christ willingly conformed to God's will. They both knew it was the only way to safeguard the law and make continued freedom possible. God is bound when we do what He says (see D&C 82:10), but when we don't, God is equally bound—not to bless, but to allow us that freedom to choose.

The debt Jesus paid was not some abstract or symbolic requirement made up by God (or by a capitalistic church). It was a very real debt to the law of justice. Law demands a penalty for sin that must be paid (see Romans 6:23). Jesus' sacrifice was not made to pacify a vengeful God. Had God the Father been able to die for us Himself, He would have. But He already had an immortal body and could not die. It had to be Jesus. The law of justice, which cares nothing for us personally, was not concerned with who suffered, only that the disrupted scales be balanced, consequences administered, and order restored. Jesus, who does care deeply for us personally, was willing to pay that penalty with His blood and thus bought our freedom. Very appropriately we sing in a sacrament hymn:

The law was broken; Jesus died
That justice might be satisfied,
That man might not remain a slave
("While of These Emblems We Partake,"
Hymns, *no. 174)*

We now stand "in the liberty wherewith Christ hath made us free" (Galatians 5:1)—not because a human suffered to appease an angry God, but because a loving God suffered to appease justice and ensure freedom.

Now that same Jesus moves beyond safeguarding freedom to helping us use and expand that freedom by calling for our obedience. President Boyd K. Packer said, "Obedience—that which God will never take by force—He will accept when freely given. And He will then return to you freedom that you can hardly dream of—the freedom to feel and to know, the freedom to do, and the freedom to *be*, at least a thousandfold more than we offer Him. Strangely enough, the key to freedom is obedience" (*That All May Be Edified*, 256–57). Elder M. Russell Ballard confirmed this when he taught, "Although freedom always brings with it certain risks, challenges, and responsibilities, it also brings real power to those who choose to exercise it wisely" (*Counseling with Our Councils*, 25).

Perhaps we are all too quick to make God the enemy. We read scriptures such as Isaiah 53:10, "It pleased [the Father] to bruise him," and we think God delighted in Jesus' suffering. We read D&C 29:5, "I am your advocate with the Father," or D&C 38:4, "pleaded before the Father for them," and we assume God is the one who desires our condemnation and must be placated. If that is the case, we will find ourselves murmuring as did Laman and Lemuel "because they knew not the dealings of that God who had created them" (1 Nephi 2:12).

We read, "Ye should work out your salvation with fear before God" (Alma 34:37) without remembering that *fear* can also mean reverence and respect. We read of the "wrath" and "anger" of God (Deuteronomy 6:15; Ephesians 5:6; Mosiah 3:26) without remembering that mercy is not made possible by removing justice but by sustaining it. To the spiritually mature, justice itself is—in the long run—a demonstration of mercy. Heavenly Father's commandments, demands, standards, and strictness, which are seen by so many as evidence that He is uncompassionate and unkind, are ultimately evidence of His love and caring for us.

For those with eyes to see, God's love is found not only in the ark but also in the flood. It is found not only in His raising the city of Enoch but also in His destroying Sodom and Gomorrah. I once could only see that through such acts of justice God was being merciful to yet unborn spirits waiting in the premortal existence. But now I can see God was also being merciful to the wicked who were taken to another place where they still had the opportunity to make better choices and progress.

God is not interested in what will make Him likable or more popular in the moment. He is concerned only with what is best. When men choose to see God as the enemy, it is only because they do not yet see His eternal perspective or His eternal purpose. The Book of Mormon teaches that God and Jesus do not do "anything save it be for the benefit of the world; for [they love] the world" (2 Nephi 26:24). Alma quotes Zenock who said, "Thou art angry, O Lord, with this people, because *they will not understand thy mercies* which thou hast bestowed upon them because of thy Son" (Alma 33:16; emphasis added).

When I was a young father struggling to balance the demands of school with work, callings, and raising my family, I sometimes found myself feeling overwhelmed. One day I read in the scriptures about the foreknowledge of God—He knows the end from the beginning (see Abraham 2:8; Helaman 8:8)—and the thought bothered me a great deal. I kept thinking that if all things were present before His eyes, then that meant God knew right then how my life would turn out. He knew whether or not I would enter the celestial kingdom, but sadly, I assumed I would not.

Maybe my discouragement was just because I was trying to juggle so many balls, or maybe it was regrets about my past. Perhaps it was just that I had gained weight and felt discouraged at my lack of self-control. Whatever the reason, I assumed I would never be able to be the kind of person who could live with God in the celestial kingdom, so in my mind that meant Jesus' suffering for me had been in vain. I felt guilty that I had made Christ suffer needlessly. Instead of being grateful for the Atonement, I felt apologetic. I was sorry I had caused Jesus pain. I could almost picture Him being upset with me for making Him suffer when I wasn't even going to make it in the end.

I did not share these private thoughts with others. I was afraid people wouldn't understand. *I* didn't understand. The more I contemplated God's foreknowledge and my own inadequacies, I couldn't help but feel somehow God was laughing at me. I could almost imagine Him saying, "You're trying really hard right now, but you'll never be able to keep it up." I felt like a turkey trying to better his life while an amused farmer was counting down the days to Thanksgiving.

Usually I was too busy to think about these concerns, but in quiet moments when I had time to ponder, I felt a little hurt and resentful. Why was God putting me through a refiner's fire if I was not worth refining? For several months I habitually went through all the right motions, but without feeling any of the right emotions. Deep down I felt far from Heavenly Father's love, acceptance, and approval. I knew He was there, and I knew the Church was true. These things had been confirmed to me over and over. I had a testimony of the Savior and His Atonement. I didn't doubt Jesus had died for me. I just felt bad He had gone to so much trouble for seemingly nothing in my case. I didn't lack faith in God or Jesus as much as I lacked faith in myself.

I didn't express these negative thoughts to anyone. I did, however, occasionally comment to my wife, Debi, that she should have married better, and I asked my father-in-law and brother about how exactly God's foreknowledge interacts with the principle of agency. Even after the good discussions those questions prompted, I still felt insecure about my future. I imagined either God was having some good laughs as He watched me struggle along or He had totally given up on me.

I knew who I was—a child of God—but this knowledge

didn't help when I talked myself into believing I was one of His bad children. I didn't doubt God's ability to love. I just figured there were others more deserving.

I have friends who would be spurred into action if they were faced with such feelings. They would take such thoughts as a challenge and redouble their efforts in order to prove themselves. I guess I have never been quite that confident. I just felt hopeless and wanted to quit.

Finally, I could no longer hide my discouragement from my wife, who lovingly asked what was bothering me. I confided my crazy thoughts, and she assured me of her love and God's. That helped for a time and I once again turned my attention to meeting the demands of life's busy routine.

Then one night I arrived home late. Debi and the children had already gone to sleep. Without turning on the light, I quietly got ready, said my prayers, and then climbed into bed trying not to disturb Debi. When I knelt to pray I didn't pray specifically about my troubling concerns or feelings. In fact, I just offered the standard thank-thee-and-please-bless late-night prayer. But when I laid my head on the pillow there came into my mind and heart an answer to my prayer of many months. I felt God communicating with me in unspoken words: "I love you. Not only because I do, but because I am bound to."

Some may not find much comfort in that thought, but for me it was a realization that brought tremendous relief, peace, and security. God is bound to love me. It is his nature to love perfectly and infinitely. He is bound to love me—not because *I* am good, but because *He* is good. Love is so central to His character that the scriptures actually say, "God *is* love" (1 John 4:8, 16; emphasis added). No matter how deficient and beyond recovery I thought I was, God was bound to love me. No matter how many balls I had juggled and let fall, no matter how much weight I had gained, how much lack of self-control I demonstrated, and how many regrets I carried from the past, He was bound to love me. No matter what my future might turn out to be, He is bound to love me. Not only did He require me to have faith and confidence in Him, but He is required to have faith and confidence in me. No foreknowledge can stop Him from investing His all in each moment, just as no foreknowledge stopped Christ from investing His all in Gethsemane and Calvary. Earth life is not merely a way of proving myself to them, but also a way for them to prove their love to me. God and Jesus are bound to believe in me—in my potential and possibilities—even when I don't. God is bound to be as close to me as He is to any of His children because He is a perfect parent. If I fail, it will not be because He has. And knowing He has not failed gives me the power I need to succeed.

It was a moment of insight that sent tears rolling from my eyes to my ears as I lay in bed. Soon I could no longer hear because my ears plugged up like they do in a swimming pool. I just lay there quietly in the dark feeling this wonderful Spirit.

Elder Jeffrey R. Holland wrote, "Just because God is God, just because Christ is Christ, they cannot do other than care for us and bless us and help us if we will but come unto them, approaching their throne of grace in meekness and lowliness of heart. They can't help but bless us. They have to. It is their nature" (*Trusting Jesus*, 68).

God loves me just as He loves His living prophets. I am one of the reasons for living prophets. God loves me just as He loves Joseph Smith. I am one of the reasons for the Restoration. God loves me just as He loves Jesus. I am one of the reasons for the Atonement. God loves people of every era just as He loved the people to whom Christ was sent in the meridian of time. Alma asked, "Is not a soul at this time as precious unto God as a soul . . . at the time of his coming?" (Alma 39:17). Paul assured us that *nothing* can separate us from the love of God (see Romans 8:35–39). Jesus Himself said to ancient Israel, "Can a woman forget her sucking child, that she should not have compassion on the son of her womb? yea, they may forget, yet will I not forget thee" (Isaiah 49:15).

God is not the enemy. He obeys laws to preserve my freedom. He is bound to. Beyond this, He is also bound to love me as I learn to use that freedom. In the Doctrine and Covenants we read that if a parent doesn't teach a child before he is accountable, the sin is upon the head of the parent (see D&C 68:25). If God doesn't "lead me, guide me, walk beside me," if He doesn't "help me find the way" (*Hymns*, no. 301), I could blame my poor choices and sins on Him, and He would never allow that to happen.

President Boyd K. Packer has said, "Had agency come to man without the Atonement, it would have been a fatal gift" (*Let Not Your Heart Be Troubled*, 80). In the same way, if the

Atonement had come to man without love, it would have been our fault rather than our freedom.

That night of personal revelation was a turning point for me. Since then, as overwhelmed as I sometimes feel, I know things will work out in time. God will not forget me—nor can He. His heart can't and won't let go. Through all the highs and lows I've experienced since that night, I have always felt safety and security as I continue going through the refining process—a process He *wouldn't* put me through if I were not worth refining. I know it will take time, but I'll get there. I have hope because I have choice.

"And now remember, remember, my brethren, that whosoever perisheth, perisheth unto himself; and whosoever doeth iniquity, doeth it unto himself; for behold, ye are free; ye are permitted to act for yourselves; for behold, God hath given unto you a knowledge and he hath made you free" (Helaman 14:30).

When I betray God's trust and use my freedom to make wrong choices, Jesus offers repentance—and the ensuing refinement. God is not laughing at me. He is loving me and lifting me. Joseph Smith taught, "And lastly, but not less important to the exercise of faith in God, is the idea that he is love. . . . When the idea is planted in the mind that he is love, who cannot see the just ground that men . . . have to exercise faith in God so as to obtain to eternal life" (*Lectures on Faith*, 3:24). I have hope because I have choice, and I can make choices with security because I have Jesus, and I have Jesus because I am loved.

If God compromised my freedom by forcing me to be good,

then not only would justice and mercy be upset but love would be lost. By allowing freedom and helping me outgrow the desire to make poor choices, the balance of justice and mercy is maintained and love grows ever stronger. It is a harder road, but it is the only one worth traveling because, while much is endured, love is preserved.

In Moses 7:30 we read, "Thou art just; thou art merciful and [thou art] kind forever." In the sacrament hymn "How Great the Wisdom and the Love" (*Hymns*, no. 195), we sing:

How great, how glorious, how complete,
Redemption's grand design,
Where justice, love, and mercy meet
In harmony divine!

Justice and mercy must be perfectly balanced to ensure freedom, but only when I learned they are balanced on a fulcrum of love did I feel hope instead of discouragement, security instead of fear. Just as God cannot and will not take away freedom, He cannot and will not ever stop loving us.

God is not the enemy. Justice is not the enemy. And we are not the enemies for putting Jesus and God through so much. Satan is the enemy (see Moroni 7:12). Lucifer is focused on our complete and utter destruction. Had he succeeded in the premortal world in taking away our freedom, our progress would have been blocked. Had he succeeded in stopping Christ's Atonement, we could never obtain resurrected bodies or repent, and our spirits would be subject to him. Had he succeeded in stopping the Restoration, the authority to perform essential ordinances would have been unavailable. No one could have been redeemed or perfected.

God and Christ have been victorious and Satan and his followers have been thwarted at each essential turning point except one—the turning point in our individual lives. Satan cannot undo the Creation, the Fall, the Atonement, or the Restoration. He cannot pull them down, so instead he tries to pull us down.

If in this life Satan can now convince us that we are worthless and that we can't make it to the celestial kingdom, what good is freedom? If he can block us from recognizing and receiving God's love, what good is the Atonement? If he can convince us to be angry with God and confused about Christ, what good is the Restoration? Who stands to gain by convincing the world God is the enemy? Only Satan. God is not the "meanie"—He is the means. "For God so loved the world, that he gave his only begotten Son, that whosoever believeth in him should not perish, but have everlasting life" (John 3:16).

Nothing illustrates better the continuous nature of the Atonement than God's continuous love for us, His children. Like the Atonement, we may not be able to explain how such love exists, but we can feel the effects of that love now and eternally. What is eternal life if it is not God's life? And what is God's life if it is not eternal love?

Chapter 8

EXCHANGING WILLPOWER FOR HIS POWER

God does not need our confession; we need to confess. Sin is wrong, but covering it up makes it worse because the only sins the Atonement can't reach are the unconfessed ones. . . . Confession makes problems a part of our past, while lying makes them a part of our future.

"Where there's a will, there's a way," or so the saying goes. My parents always told me, "Where there's a *Wilcox*, there's a way." Sometimes neither is the case. Even with all the will (and Wilcoxes) in the world, some people struggle for years to break bad habits. What they have yet to internalize is that success ultimately is found not in willpower, but in God's power.

Robert L. Millet wrote, "There is a better and higher motivation . . . that is above and beyond self-discipline, well beyond sheer willpower and dogged determination. It is a motivation born of the Spirit, one that comes to us as a result of a change of heart" (*Grace Works*, 89–90). This change of heart is closely linked with what Joseph Smith called the first principles and ordinances of the gospel. Those first principles and ordinances of the gospel are the means by which we accept and apply the Atonement in our lives continually—every minute of every hour of every day of every year.

My eldest son's mission president, Lindon J. Robison, had a profound impact on many lives as he served in Spain. He taught his missionaries the steps of repentance in a memorable way—by examining their opposites. Following his lead, let's consider the UN-principles of the gospel:

UN-FAITH

In place of faith in Christ, some choose disbelief. When people say, "There is no God," or, "The Church isn't true," their words can put us on the defensive. However, such comments are sometimes attempts to justify poor choices and avoid change. When we listen beyond the words, the message really being communicated in such cases is, "I've sinned and don't want to repent."

A young man who became fascinated by anti-Mormon literature had never read much in the scriptures or Church magazines, yet suddenly he was devouring entire anti-Mormon books and reading every word on anti-Mormon Web sites. He would rush to show me some obscure statement of Joseph Smith or Brigham Young—usually taken completely out of context—which "proved" they were false prophets. He anxiously reported, according to his "unbiased" sources, that "all Mormons are prejudiced" and "all Mormon males are dictatorial." I recognized the statements as unsupported generalizations, but he heard only what he wanted to hear.

One day after speaking with him at length about the exaggerations and lies he was accepting so willingly, I said to him, "In my experience, when people are anxious to prove the Church wrong it is sometimes because they are trying to cover their sins." The young man protested and said he couldn't believe I would think such a thing. He criticized me for being judgmental. However, within the week he confessed serious problems with morality.

This young man did not really have genuine questions or doubts about the Church, its leaders, or its history. He just wanted to soothe his conscience. He figured if the members or standards of the Church could be shown to be wrong, he could feel justified. He thought if he could conveniently make God disappear, he could in "good conscience" do whatever he wanted. Like the wicked Nephites in the Book of Mormon, he sought his own "prophet" who would tell him, "There is no iniquity. . . . Do whatsoever your heart desireth" (Helaman 13:27). In time he learned he was better off putting his efforts into altering himself rather than trying to alter truth.

On another occasion a woman asked, "What does it matter if I choose not to believe in God? That doesn't affect anyone." Although not directly, her choice *does* affect others because disbelief in God is also an expression of disbelief in people. Rejecting God and Christ is a declaration that potential is limited. Self-betterment becomes a futile exercise at best, an impossibility at worst. Choosing to live without faith in Christ is choosing to admit defeat and surrender hope. To live "without God in the world" is to be "in a state contrary to the nature of happiness" (Alma 41:11). On the other hand, as we choose faith in Christ we are not only recognizing His perfection, but acknowledging the possibilities that lie within all of us.

I once spoke at a lockdown facility for young people dealing with everything from drug problems and sexual addictions to extreme violent behavior. After the presentation I greeted these young people and looked into their eyes. I saw more hope in some than in others. As the program director escorted me out of the building, I asked, "What makes the difference?"

He explained, "Some have just been here longer." He then provided some impressive statistics supporting the success of his program over time.

"Obviously, you are helping these young people in wonderful ways," I said. "But do the changes last once they leave?"

The director smiled, looked around to make sure we were alone, and then said quietly, "Only if they connect with God." He explained that post-program research showed that those who had had spiritual experiences were much more likely to make enduring changes than those who hadn't.

Amulek spoke of those who "connect with God" as having "faith unto repentance" (Alma 34:15–17). "Only unto him that has faith unto repentance is brought about the great and eternal plan of redemption" (Alma 34:16). True faith in Christ is more than a declaration of belief or hope. It leads to action.

UN-HUMILITY

The first step in the repentance process is humility. The opposite is pride. Some show pride by rejecting God. Others show pride by rejecting the need to change, insisting that God and Christ must tolerate their sins. Humility recognizes how different we are from Christ and helps us desire to make that difference less apparent. Pride erases the need for change by magnifying our self-image or diminishing Christ to the point we see no reason to strive for improvement. Pride sees repentance as undeserved humiliation and punishment. Humility sees it as a way to turn away from sin and toward God. No wonder scriptures speak about the constant need for meekness, lowliness (see Moroni 7:43), and "a broken heart and a contrite spirit" (2 Nephi 2:7). The Atonement must be used to escape sin and be comfortable with God rather than trying to escape God and be comfortable with sin.

Truman G. Madsen told of the pride he encountered among some of his associates as they examined the Church. He wrote, "From renowned figures in the world, including some notoriously secular, and in many languages, I have heard whispers of genuine envy. This from people who know enough to know that Latter-day Saints are onto something, but who just can't stand the cost of embracing that something" ("Man Against Darkness," 42). Sadly, even members of the Church who know full well that Latter-day Saints are "onto something" still can't stand the "cost of embracing" it. And what is the "cost" that seems to be holding so many back? It always starts with letting go of pride.

UN-RECOGNITION

Also essential to repentance is recognizing our weaknesses. Un-recognition declares that sin is not sin and demands that everyone accept us just as we are. God can do little with the unwilling and rebellious. A Japanese proverb states, "A problem clearly identified is half the solution"; un-recognition keeps us from identifying the problem. As I spoke to one man about his pornography addiction, he responded, "It's not an addiction. It's just harmless entertainment—no different from walking through an art museum." He claimed he felt no remorse for his actions—at least, that was what he publicly claimed. However, years later, he came to me privately and in tears sought help. He knew his choices had affected not only himself but all those he loved and who loved him.

Such realizations take time. It is often difficult to distinguish between truth and the many worldly views and opinions that so constantly bombard us. There are plenty of voices that present good to be evil and evil to be good. Selfishness is described as a virtue and selflessness as a vice. Still, deep down we know right from wrong.

Elder M. Russell Ballard said, "Make no mistake about it: We know when we are not doing what we ought to do because every one of us has a conscience. We are born with the light of Christ, and we know instinctively what is right and what is wrong when it comes to our personal behavior" (*When Thou Art Converted*, 121–22).

Most of us try to avoid touching a hot stove, but if it happens we recognize the problem and withdraw our hand quickly. The pain prompts swift action, which keeps us from damaging ourselves further. Who among us is going to leave his hand on the stove and try to convince himself it doesn't really hurt? Committing sin is like touching a hot stove. In normal cases, the pain of guilt leads to recognition, which leads to quick repentance (see Packer, "The Touch of the Master's Hand," 23). This is exactly what Alma taught when he said, "Let your sins trouble you, with that trouble which shall bring you down unto repentance" (Alma 42:29). Un-recognition leads only to anger and defiance, which in turn lead to justification. Instead of looking for help, we look for excuses.

In the context of touching a hot stove, consider some of the most common excuses for sin:

Just one touch won't hurt.

I'm afraid if I take my hand off I won't be able to leave it off.

I deserve this.

The only reason I feel pain is because of my Mormon culture.

But I was born with the desire to touch the stove.

It's my parents' fault. They're the ones who bought the stove.

I just need to adjust to the burning rather than try to overcome it.

I want to be excommunicated so it won't hurt when I touch the stove.

No one told me touching the hot stove was bad.

It may hurt, but at least I am touching it with someone I love.

It's not like it's totally wrong. It's a gray area.

Everyone else is touching it.

I'll touch it if I want. It's my right. Nobody is going to tell me what to do or not do.

Stove? What stove? I don't see any stove.

I just don't care anymore. I'm numb to it.

I know it's wrong, but I'll move my hand tomorrow.

You can't go without touching the stove all the time.

I've blown it now. I might as well touch it more.

Those who don't touch are so old-fashioned.

At least it's just my hand and not my whole face.

How will I know it hurts unless I touch it myself?

At least the other stove touchers accept me and don't judge.

There are others who touch it more than I do.

If God didn't want me to touch the stove, He wouldn't have given me a hand.

Obviously, it is easier to find excuses than it is to find God, but excuses can't sustain us the way God does. They can't help us the way He can, and they certainly can't love us. "Do not endeavor to excuse yourself in the least point because of your sins" (Alma 42:30).

UN-REMORSE

Avoiding sin is not always as easy as avoiding a hot stove because sin can often appeal to our carnal natures and become an acquired appetite as strong as—if not stronger than—hunger. This makes the thought of change virtually overwhelming.

Those who take responsibility for their choices usually feel godly sorrow for their wrongful actions. By contrast, those who don't accept this responsibility generally feel bad only when they think they might get caught.

A former missionary, upon returning home, allowed himself to slip back into bad habits. He was brokenhearted. He had expected so much more of himself. As he looked at his reflection in the mirror, he felt nothing but self-loathing. At every Church meeting he attended he felt self-conscious. It seemed every talk, every lesson was directed at him. At this low point, he wrote the following poem in his journal:

When you allow yourself to go too far,
When you make no effort to bridle your passion,
When you fall from grace, your innocence lost,
Beauty fades from your face as you slip from your
place.
Oh the guilt—enough to start your own religion.
Discouragement reigns.
You begin to count the days since you last felt of worth
You rationalize as you long to keep your place in a
society
That has little tolerance for misbehavers—
Even those who wish to be counted among the
believers.
So you determine to let what is private stay private
Since you've already opened the floodgates of
allowance and given in,
Since you've already committed those awful crimes
Against the very beliefs that are supposedly the fiber of
your being,
Since you've got a new scarlet letter to wear,
You might as well earn it well by continuing to
indulge,
To grant path to your passion

For you are already a criminal.
Your progress is stopped though you are still yet to be caught by the system.
How careful you are that your filth should not be discovered.
You protect your little secret with a series of barriers filled with half-truths.
You long for normalcy; to fit actions to the morals you were taught.
For those are your truth and your testimony,
Your inner light cries out for them
For it knows your purpose and longs for you to fulfill your destiny.
Your spirit longs to complete this journey with honor,
All the while fighting against its worst enemy—
The very thing closest to it—
Your body.
The constant battle with the natural man rages on.
You find yourself with the worst kind of sickness—
Addiction.

The powerful and personal words of this returned missionary explained how he was feeling, but he knew they didn't excuse how he was feeling. Sin—even when wrapped in the tentacles of addiction—is always a choice. Now he determined to let his remorse lead him to begin again to make better choices. Even though it seemed impossible, he knew it wasn't. President Boyd K. Packer taught, "It is contrary to the order of heaven for any soul to be locked into compulsive, immoral behavior with no way out!" ("Little Children," 18).

This returned missionary read Isaiah 40:26–31 and Matthew 24. The words gave him courage to meet with his bishop and begin—once again—the repentance process. He knew recovery was a long road. He had traveled it before, but in a strange way even that gave him hope. From his own experience he knew remorse could pave the way for joy. If Christ helped him once, He would help him again. He assumed he had already put off the "natural man" and become a "saint" through the Atonement (Mosiah 3:19) as he prepared to serve a full-time mission. Now he realized that even saints have to keep putting off the natural man over and over again—a process made possible through the Atonement. If it was there for him in the past, it would be there for him now.

UN-CONFESSION

The opposite of confessing is hiding. Mark Twain wrote, "A person does a low-down thing, and then he don't want to take no consequences of it. Thinks as long as he can hide, it ain't no disgrace" (*Adventures of Huckleberry Finn*, 227).

Satan's advice to Adam and Eve when they discovered their nakedness was to hide. It is the same thing he tells each of us when we realize we have sinned. Could trees hide Adam and Eve? Could their fig-leaf aprons? (see Moses 4:13–14). No more than our silence, avoidance, and procrastination can conceal our deeds and thoughts from the all-seeing eyes of God.

God does not need our confession; we need to confess. Sin is wrong, but covering it up makes it worse because the only sins the Atonement can't reach are the unconfessed ones. When a woman reached out to touch the hem of Christ's robe, Jesus asked, "Who touched me?" (Mark 5:30–33). Although the woman's act was not a sin, she still felt fear about admitting the truth and being found out. Nevertheless, she faced her fear, came forward, and only then was able to hear the words for which her heart longed: "Go in peace."

"He that covereth his sins shall not prosper; but whoso confesseth and forsaketh them shall have mercy" (Proverbs 28:13). Speaking in the current dispensation the Lord said, "I . . . forgive sins unto those who confess their sins" (D&C 64:7). In addition to the Lord's forgiveness, this vital demonstration of godly sorrow allows us to obtain forgiveness from the Church and receive help, counsel, and guidance in making changes. Confession makes problems a part of our past, while lying makes them a part of our future.

Honest people can't be content with a partial confession—saying something happened only once when it happened more often, or saying it was long ago when it was more recent. "Do ye imagine to yourselves that ye can lie unto the Lord?" (Alma 5:17). Telling only some of our sins, our most recent or socially acceptable sins, or disguising the seriousness or frequency of our problems does little good.

Some people don't feel worthy to participate fully in the gospel because they are not completely free of bad habits. Although that freedom is our long-term goal, for now our worthiness can be defined as being completely honest with priesthood leaders, and making progress in the right direction. There is no place for sin in heaven. There is a place for sinners who are willing to confess, learn from mistakes, sincerely progress through a repentance process, and welcome the power of the Atonement.

One young man wrote the following to me upon entering the Missonary Training Center: "It was amazing how Satan would keep trying to make me feel bad about the past. He would whisper, 'You're not worthy to be here.' The only thing that got me through was knowing that I had put everything out on the table. My confession was complete. I would think, *Satan, there is NOTHING my priesthood leader doesn't know, and if he says I am worthy, I'm worthy. HE is the judge in Israel, not YOU.*"

Two people can commit the same sin and one can be found worthy and the other not: The difference is a repentant attitude and the willingness to try to improve. Perfection isn't our immediate goal. Progress is. Elder Bruce C. Hafen has said that developing a Christlike character "requires patience and persistence more than it requires flawlessness" (*Broken Heart*, 186). Sincere desire and effort to improve—however slow our progress may be—can qualify us to worthily partake of the sacrament sitting right alongside people who have never experienced our individual struggles. As we set short-term goals together with priesthood leaders, they can help us reach those goals and determine our next steps. This positive process allows us to celebrate mini-milestones and build on a series of triumphs rather than failures.

It takes time to get our lives tangled up. We can't expect

them to be unraveled in a single day. Mark Twain also wrote, "Habit is habit, and not to be flung out of the window by any man, but coaxed downstairs a step at a time" (*Pudd'nhead Wilson*, 45). President Spencer W. Kimball put it even more clearly when he wrote, "Certainly self-mastery is a continuous program—a journey, not a single start" (*Miracle of Forgiveness*, 210).

In an effort to better empathize with investigators as they try to conquer addictions, missionaries are encouraged to think of a habit they have—something they do frequently, without thinking, such as cracking their knuckles, adjusting their glasses, eating too much, or sleeping too late—and then go one day without doing those things, then a week, and so forth (see *Preach My Gospel*, 190). This step-by-step approach can work for missionaries, investigators, and everyone. However, it works best when bishops and others who support us can help hold us accountable and track our progress. That's why it is vital we go to them.

UN-RESTITUTION

Repentance requires making amends to those we have harmed or betrayed and finding ways to make things right. The opposite is to seek ways around such restitution. As a teacher I have received letters from former students apologizing for cheating on a test or giving themselves undeserved credit on a self-evaluated task. Also I have received letters from former students who confess their participation in some childhood or adolescent prank, asking how they can repair the damage. Do I think less of those students? No. Absolutely not. I am not ashamed of them. On the contrary, I am thrilled they have finally reached the point in their spiritual progression where they care more about what God thinks of them than what I or anyone else thinks.

In some cases, such as sexual misconduct, it is impossible to restore that which has been taken. However, there is amazing power in the words, *I'm sorry*. Nothing moves both giver and receiver forward like a sincere apology. In these situations we can't backtrack and repair the damage. That is work for the Savior. But an apology opens the door for everyone involved to feel the Savior's healing influence.

In some cases, restitution can include an informal or formal probation, disfellowshipment, or even, in the most extreme and/or public of cases, excommunication. All such actions entail a postponement of certain privileges of Church membership to one degree or other. Nevertheless, in all circumstances these steps are taken in a spirit of love and concern.

UN-COVENANTS

"In a covenant—a two-way promise—the Lord agrees to do for us what we could never do for ourselves—forgive our sins, lift our burdens, renew our souls, and re-create our nature, raise us from the dead, and qualify us for glory hereafter. At the same time, we promise to . . . receive the ordinances of salvation, love and serve one another, and do all in our power to put off the natural man and deny ourselves of ungodliness" (Millet, *Grace Works*, 116).

The opposite of covenants with God are promises or commitments made to ourselves, which are easily broken, postponed, or forgotten. Commitments to others can be more helpful—especially to another person who loves us and cares deeply for us. It's fairly obvious that a person who arranges to exercise with a valued friend usually hangs in there longer than someone who does not. When the alarm goes off in the morning, it's easy to turn it off and roll over unless we know that someone we care about—and who genuinely cares about us—is waiting. But even these commitments to others can falter under pressure.

Covenants are different. They remove any illusion we may have about our own ability and lead us to acknowledge our dependence on God. They allow us to tap divine power because "the promises he makes to us always include the power to grow in our capacity to keep covenants" (Eyring, "Child of God," 46). Making promises to ourselves or even to others is like putting water in a gas tank. Sure, it fills the tank, but it will not get us to our final destination. Only by making *covenants* can we find the proper fuel—the power—that makes a difference. Covenants connect us to Christ, who said, "I will not leave you comfortless: I will come to you" (John 14:18).

Covenants are not merely a contract or an if/then deal. "Those who enter into the covenants of the gospel of Jesus Christ also enter a precious and ongoing relationship with the Savior, by which he nourishes them with personal and spiritual sustenance" (Hafen and Hafen, *Belonging Heart,* 113). "Our faith and our repentance qualify us to enter that relationship, just as the Savior's Atonement qualifies him to enter it. . . . This relationship becomes the medium by which the unlimited range of the Atonement's blessings begins its everlasting flow" (*Belonging Heart,* 152).

In the temple, as covenants are made, Jesus symbolically holds our hands tighter and tighter until we are finally held so firmly it is almost impossible to break the grasp. Such symbols teach us about accessing Christ's power through covenants.

Patricia T. Holland said, "What we too often fail to realize is that at the same time we covenant with God, He is covenanting with us—promising blessings, privileges, and pleasures our eyes have not yet seen and our ears have not yet heard. Though we may see our part in the matter of faithfulness going by fits and starts, bumps and bursts, our progress erratic at best, God's part is sure and steady and supreme. We may stumble, but He never does. We may falter, but He never will. We may feel out of control, but He never is. . . . Covenants forge a link between our telestial, mortal struggles and God's celestial, immortal powers ("God's Covenant of Peace," 372–73).

For many years I did not understand Sister Holland's beautiful perspective. I looked at my end of covenant keeping as the way that I earned eternal life. I figured that immortality was free, but eternal life had to be earned. Now I realize that both are free (see D&C 6:13; 14:7), but eternal life must be received by faith in Christ, which includes covenants and the ordinances that evidence those covenants (D&C 88:33). A drowning person doesn't earn a life preserver. He can only choose to refuse it or to accept it (see Bytheway, *SOS*, 62–63). When it comes to the Atonement, Christ didn't deserve what He got, and we certainly don't deserve what He gave.

Elder Jeffrey R. Holland wrote, "Obviously the unconditional blessings of the Atonement are unearned, but the conditional ones are not fully merited either. By living faithfully and keeping the commandments of God, one can receive additional privileges; but they are still given freely, not technically earned" ("Atonement of Jesus Christ," 36).

Making covenants is not a way to earn a free gift, but rather a way to learn how to accept that gift freely and gratefully. We do not keep covenants in order to prove ourselves worthy of grace, but rather to improve upon that which is given (see Matthew 25:20–23) and thereby grow in grace (see 2 Peter 3:18). When we speak of the human part of a covenant as something we can do without God's assistance, or the divine part of a covenant as something we can repay, we not only grossly overestimate our abilities but we also see the arrangement as a one-time deal. When we fully realize the continuous nature of the Atonement, gratitude and obedience are less a condition for receiving it and more a natural outgrowth of it. They become as continuous as the gift itself. In that moment, we realize we do not earn the Atonement. The Atonement actually earns us.

UN-SPIRIT

When we enjoy the Holy Ghost, we enjoy light, happiness, peace, protection, and all gifts of the Spirit. The opposite includes darkness, discouragement, frustration, and fear.

I once spoke with a woman who had left the Church and was no longer maintaining LDS standards. I asked her how she reconciled her present lifestyle with her testimony. She said, "I don't have a testimony. I never did."

I asked, "You mean during all the prayers, scriptures, firesides, seminary classes, EFYs, and Young Women's camps when you were growing up, you *never* felt the Spirit?"

She responded, "What I felt was emotion. I just made up those feelings."

"Then make them up again—right now. Hurry. If you have the power to make up feelings like that, do it again," I urged.

She said, "I can't."

I agreed. "You can't now, and you couldn't back then, either. The Spirit can't be manipulated like that. You have felt the Spirit. You just need to remember it and let the feelings lead you back to God."

We are all dependent on the Spirit to help us in our quest to break bad habits and improve our lives. B. H. Roberts taught: "Even after the sins of the past are forgiven, the one so pardoned will doubtless feel the force of sinful habits bearing heavily upon him. . . . There is an absolute necessity for some additional sanctifying grace that will strengthen poor human nature. . . . Man's natural powers are unequal to this task. . . . Such strength, such power, such a sanctifying grace is conferred on man in being born of the Spirit—in receiving the Holy Ghost" (*Gospel and Man's Relationship to Deity*, 179–80).

Jesus commands all the "ends of the earth" to be baptized in water "that ye may be sanctified by the reception of the Holy Ghost, that ye may stand spotless before me at the last day" (3 Nephi 27:20). Spotlessness does not come just in the moment of baptism, but as the Holy Ghost sanctifies us throughout our lives. "Sanctification is an ongoing process, and we obtain that glorious status by degrees as we overcome the world and become saints in deed as well as in name" (McConkie, *New Witness*, 266).

UN-ENDURANCE

The opposite of enduring "all the remainder of our days" (Mosiah 5:5) and pressing "forward with a steadfastness in Christ" (2 Nephi 31:20) is giving up. Too many become discouraged by the painstakingly slow process of sanctification and decide to toss in the towel. In such low moments, we surprise ourselves by how quickly we can slip backward even when we have sworn before God, angels, and witnesses that we wouldn't. We shouldn't be surprised, however, at how quickly Christ comes to our aid if we seek Him. "When [Peter] saw the wind boisterous, he was afraid; and beginning to sink, he cried, saying, Lord, save me. And *immediately* Jesus stretched forth his hand and caught him" (Matthew 14:30–31; emphasis added).

God, who will not be mocked, does extend a hand to

mockers who repent. Trying and slipping and trying again is not mocking God as much as it is honoring Him. Satan claims to hold covenant breakers in his power. But what power does he have in and of himself? He has power only if we give it to him. He can't stop us from determining to start again. Christ's broken heart is more powerful than our broken promises and Satan's blustering and empty threats.

When I slip, instead of saying "I have failed," I try to say "I have not yet succeeded." Instead of saying "Look how far there is to go," I try to say "Look how far God and Christ have brought me." Instead of saying "I can't keep my covenants," I try to say "I can't do it now, but with heaven's help I can learn." Instead of saying "I can't walk on water," I try to say "At least I got out of the boat!" In scripture we learn that even Christ "received not of the fulness at first . . . but continued from grace to grace, until he received a fulness" (D&C 93:12–13). Can we expect our progress to be quicker?

There is a Spanish saying: *Sin prisa, pero sin pausa.* ("Without great hurry, but also without a pause.") In English we might say, "Slow and steady wins the race." We don't have to reach our goals by Friday. We have till Sunday and then the next Sunday and the next—each time we have the opportunity to partake of the sacrament. Enduring to the end does not necessarily mean living without errors. Enduring to the end means enduring in the covenant despite errors.

Whenever we return to the temple, we do the work for someone else, but each time we partake of the sacrament, it is always for us. Participating in this ordinance repeatedly is one way we progress from grace to grace, or from a bestowal of grace to a bestowal of grace. Some appropriately define "grace to grace" as progressing through levels, but I like to also think of it as an expression of the continuous nature of grace.

In sacred sacrament moments can we really promise to never again make a mistake? Not when we know full well we will be back again the very next week needing the sacrament as much as ever. Rather, we show we are *willing* to take upon ourselves His name, *willing* to always remember Him, and *willing* to keep His commandments (see Moroni 4:3; D&C 46:9). As we renew covenants, we are committing not to be perfect *like* Christ immediately but to be perfected *in* Christ over time.

"Behold, ye are little children and ye cannot bear all things now; ye must grow in grace" (D&C 50:40). This is the growth process King Benjamin called retaining a remission of our sins "from day to day" (Mosiah 4:12, 26), or we could say from Sunday to Sunday. Enduring to the end doesn't seem so overwhelming when we break decades and years into smaller measurements and just take life one week at a time. The sacrament is our most continuous catalyst to enduring.

A woman learning English as a second language once paid me the supreme compliment. She told me she thought I was Christlike. Unfortunately, what I heard was "cross-eyed." I couldn't understand why she would say such a thing. Finally her real intent became clear. Although humbled and deeply honored, I nevertheless felt that my first impression was more accurate. Most days we all probably feel more cross-eyed than Christlike. During such times, we can find comfort in recalling the words of President James E. Faust, "I am grateful that it is never too late to change, to make things right, to leave old activities and habits behind" ("Unwanted Messages," 10). Because of the continuous Atonement, it's never too late to exchange willpower for God's power.

Chapter 9

FAITH WITHOUT WORKS (AND WORKS WITHOUT SUPERVISION)

God wants our obedience and sacrifice, but only as a means to an end. He wants us to live the gospel, but even this is still a means to an end. What He ultimately wants from all of us is exactly that—all of us. He wants our consecration.

If "faith without works is dead" (James 2:20), then works without proper motives are in Intensive Care. Anyone can work when being supervised. If Mom, Dad, teacher, or leader is watching, even slackers can act like they are doing their best. The key is to be working with the same intensity even when no one is looking. That's what Paul noticed and complimented in some of the early Saints when he wrote, "Wherefore, my beloved, as ye have always obeyed, not as in my presence only, but now much more in my absence" (Philippians 2:12).

In 1939, near the end of the Great Depression, Channing Pollock wrote *The Adventures of a Happy Man: Work Is Its Own Reward.* In it he explained that the unhappiest people are those who are lazy and fight boredom, while the happiest are those who learn to work. He also pointed out that the best work is never done for a paycheck. It gets done by those who believe in what they are doing.

Members of the Church of Jesus Christ know a lot about believing in what we are doing. We know a lot about working in the Church without any thought of a paycheck. However, we are still working at various levels of motivation (see Oaks, *Pure in Heart*, 37–49). Some work because they feel it is required, others because they feel it is expected, but hopefully most work because of righteous desires.

PERCEIVED REQUIREMENTS

Two missionaries were overheard talking in the Missionary Training Center after a particularly challenging week. "So why did you come?" one asked. "And don't tell me you wanted to share the happiness of the gospel with others."

"Honestly," the other said, "my dad promised me he would pay for school if I came."

"You're lucky," said the first. "My dad would just thrash me if I didn't."

The promise of extrinsic rewards can motivate us to do a lot of things. Fear of punishment can also motivate. Although I seriously doubt any dad is going to "thrash" a son for not serving a mission, obviously the fear of a father's reaction can weigh heavily on a son's mind. No one wants to get in trouble or have a privilege revoked. We take out the garbage and pay our rent on time because we don't want to face the penalties.

Although punishments do influence us, they are not good long-term motivators. It is the same with rewards. Any parent who has ever tried to encourage a child to get good grades by offering money realizes how quickly the motivation fades. Soon the time involved in the deal has to be shortened or the amount of money has to be increased.

Fortunately, not many members of the Church serve just because we are promised a reward or because we hope to avoid a punishment—even eternally. Most have moved to higher levels of motivation.

PERCEIVED EXPECTATIONS

A measure of work in the Church gets done because of perceived expectations. We're not getting prizes or being threatened, but we do sometimes feel a sharp sense of duty or social pressure. One young elder told his MTC branch president, "Coming on this mission is the scariest thing I have ever done. I am shy and don't like to talk to people in English—let alone in another language. But I knew I needed to do it. I knew my bishop and parents would be disappointed if I didn't come."

Although much can be accomplished at this level of motivation, it doesn't always leave us feeling very spiritually satisfied. For example, a ward member sits on the back row of a fast and testimony meeting. The counselor to the bishop begins to speak: "I love this gospel," he says with great emotion. Listening, the ward member in the back says to himself, "Why don't I feel what he is feeling?"

The two of them might be in the same room, but they are probably there for different reasons. The one in the back has come perhaps out of perceived obligation—he or she "should" be there. The one in the front may be feeling a higher level of motivation: He is there because he wants to be—because he loves it. As the saying goes, they both get out of it what they put into it.

RIGHTEOUS DESIRES

All those who hope to find a treasure in heaven will do so by learning to treasure heavenly things. No one will stay in the celestial kingdom because he or she "has to" or should.

For some, family history is a chore, a job, a responsibility. They would need to be offered a lot of rewards before they would dig through and organize old family records. Others might do it if they heard an especially good talk that made them feel especially guilty. For my dad, family history work was a passion. Dad found joy and satisfaction in family history. He literally had to be pulled away from it.

Some feel equally passionate about computers, animals, gardening, or sports. They invest time in these activities because they love them. Why do most of us eat ice cream? It's not because Mom is standing there saying, "You finish that whole bowl or you don't get any carrots!" Most of us do it because we love it.

As we get caught up in the happy cycle of loving what we do and doing what we love, work becomes a joy. We are not watching the clock. In fact, we forget time exists. We are working not because a supervisor is present but because we are lost in the love of it.

One missionary wrote, "President, I've fallen totally in love. Don't worry. It is not with a girl. It is with the work. I love missionary work. I just can't stop. I can't get my brain to think about anything else. I've fallen hopelessly and helplessly in love."

This elder was not counting days, baptisms, or packages; he was making all those things count for something greater. He worked without supervision, not because he was proving himself to God but because he was thanking Him.

Of course, loving what we are doing doesn't mean we are blissfully smiling and running through fields of flowers every day. My father experienced many frustrations as he pursued family history. The missionary described above still got hot in the summer and cold in the winter. He still went to bed tired and sometimes disheartened.

In the Book of Mormon we learn about those who loved God so much they had "no more disposition to do evil, but to do good continually" (Mosiah 5:2). Does this mean they were never enticed again? Surely not, since that would have limited their agency. Does this mean they never made another mistake or had another bad day? No. They probably messed up just like we do, since they were living in the same fallen world in which we live. The issue isn't whether or not they slipped, but that they didn't want to. "And, thanks be to God, we will be judged not only by our works but also by the desires of our hearts" (Millet, *Grace Works*, 55; see also Alma 41:3; D&C 137:9). The renewed people of King Benjamin probably sinned again, but they most certainly recognized it when they did and repented quickly (see D&C 109:21). They lived in a constant spirit of repentance because of their righteous desires.

MOVING THROUGH THE LEVELS

But what if we *don't* desire what is right? It is comforting to hear that the Lord looks on the heart (1 Samuel 16:7)—except when our heart desires the wrong things. If we are not careful, the natural man can quickly become more friend than foe. That which degrades can be appealing. That which destroys can be appetizing. One friend put it like this: "It's not just a constant struggle between what my spirit wants and what I've trained my body to want. That would be difficult, but beatable. My problem is I honestly desire what the Church says is wrong."

Only Jesus has the power to create a mighty change by educating our desires and turning our hearts away from evil and toward Him. In a game of darts, we may not hit the bull's-eye every time. However, we stand a better chance when we aim at the target and not the opposite wall.

Even once we are moving in the right direction, we may still be on different levels of motivation in different aspects of our lives. The Lord sometimes referred to Joseph as His servant (see D&C 1:17). At other times He called him His son (see D&C 121:7) and His friend (see D&C 93:45). No doubt even the Prophet and his associates were progressing through the levels of motivation. Servants are required to work. Sons are expected to work. However, friends work because they want to. How did Joseph and other Church leaders get to the point where they were motivated always by righteous desires? For them, as for all of us, it starts with obedience.

Most young men in the Church today don't grow up listening

to the Tabernacle Choir, awakening early, and wearing ties daily. Yet when they go on missions they are willing to do those things in order to be obedient. As they obey and make sacrifices, they begin to see reasons behind the rules. The Restoration was not simply a restoration of rules but also of reasons. "Therefore God gave unto them commandments, *after* having made known unto them the plan of redemption" (Alma 12:32; emphasis added).

As a young missionary starts understanding *why* he wakes up early and *why* he must avoid worldly music, he finds those things easier to do. As he grows in understanding and obedience, the Spirit confirms the correctness of his choices. He finds it easier to obey. Still, knowing why he needs to be friendly, set a good example, smile at strangers, and push broken-down cars doesn't mean he is going to always love what he is doing. Take eating vegetables, for instance: We know they are important. We know their benefits. Therefore, we manage to make ourselves eat them even if we do not love them initially.

We are not bad people because we have bad habits. We are good people trying to develop good habits.

How, then, do we take the leap to the highest level of motivation—really wanting to do what we're doing? It helps to be with people who have already done so. Being around righteous, happy people who love what they do can rub off on us. Having a testimony also helps. Nothing can motivate us more than knowing the truth for ourselves. However, there are lots of people who have strong testimonies and positive, faithful friends, but it is still quite a stretch for them to actually love home teaching or speaking in church.

When we're working on purifying our motives, we can consider how we made the jump to higher levels of motivation in other aspects of our lives. What have we learned to love that we didn't initially like? For some it might be listening to classical music, watching general conference, or driving a stick shift. Whatever the activity, it was not a matter of just doing it until we got used to it. It was a matter of seeing beyond the activity to something greater.

Perhaps classical music touched our emotions. Driving a stick made us feel powerful. General conference put us in close contact with the Spirit and helped us feel closer to God. As our perspective broadens, these experiences become not just items to be checked off a list, but part of who we are. With an enlarged perspective, suddenly we cannot imagine life without listening to general conference or driving a stick shift. We can't understand why everyone doesn't do these things. Perhaps we feel genuine sadness for those who are missing out. These experiences stop being ends in themselves, and become means to greater ends. This is the power of broader vision—seeing "afar off" (Genesis 22:4; Hebrews 11:13).

One of the many blessings of the temple is the expanded vision it provides. Why did God command the Saints to sacrifice and complete the Nauvoo Temple even when they were being forced to leave it behind? He knew the vision they obtained within the holy temple would give them the motivation they needed to face the trials that lay ahead. In the same way, God can provide a broader vision not only to our eyes but to our hearts.

Elder Neal A. Maxwell taught that when people fall away due to lack of self-discipline, it is because "their perspective shrinks" (*We Will Prove Them Herewith*, 26). In Elder Maxwell's biography we learned how he maintained his own self-discipline and bridled his passions: by maintaining a "sense of mission" (Hafen, *A Disciple's Life*, 289). The same God who provided that enlarged vision for the early Saints and for Elder Maxwell can and will provide it for us. Then we must cling to it and never lose it.

One young man described the growth process he went through when he learned to keep a journal. He said, "When my stake president set me apart for my mission, he challenged me to write in my journal every day." The missionary agreed and did it. At first it was just out of obedience, so he could report back to his stake president without feeling guilty. Then, while in the MTC, he was taught about the benefits of a journal—especially in his studies. The elder explained, "Their words validated what I was doing and brought new life to my efforts. I figured maybe one day my grandchildren might enjoy reading my journal." Over time, however, keeping a journal became a way to reach additional goals. Continuing, the missionary said, "My journal became a place to think and discover. When I needed to vent, I went to my journal. I didn't know what I would do without it. I realized I wasn't keeping it for my stake president or even for my future posterity. I was doing it for me because I loved it."

God wants our obedience and sacrifice, but only as a means to an end. He wants us to live the gospel, but even this is still a means to an end. What He ultimately wants from all of us is exactly that—all of us. He wants our consecration.

"Obedience is the first law of heaven," taught Joseph F. Smith (*Journal of Discourses*, 16:248). However, obedience is only the starting point that allows the rest of the climb to be possible. Is there any question that the Apostles are going to study their scriptures, listen to appropriate music, and be good examples for others? None. Why? Because they feel it's required? Because it's their job? Is it because they feel it's expected because they are being watched? No. It is because those behaviors are founded on beliefs that are at the core of who they are. These servants of heaven live consecrated lives.

Living such a life is possible for each of us. The temple endowment makes it clear that God can help us to progress through levels of motivation. Those with the Aaronic Priesthood can ultimately receive the Melchizedek Priesthood. Those in the telestial room can move to the celestial room. What begins as obedience and sacrifice can end as consecration.

THE GREATEST MOTIVATION

Why did Jesus atone for us? Was it a requirement? After all, He had been promised all the Father had. Was that reward what motivated Christ to atone for us? No. Was it a fear of punishment—the threat of endless torment and outer darkness? No.

Perhaps it was out of obligation. He was the oldest. It was His responsibility. Everyone expected him to do it. Was duty the only thing on the Savior's mind as He made His way toward the Garden of Gethsemane and the cross? No.

There is only one possible answer: Jesus didn't merely see a bigger picture; He saw the entire picture. He didn't merely see a broadened vision; he saw with perfect vision.

Did He avoid eternal punishment? Yes. Did He receive eternal rewards? Yes. But those were not his motivation. They were simply natural consequences that followed His choice at a higher level. Did He fulfill His birthright obligation? Yes. Did He please His father? Yes. But those were natural consequences as well, not motives. What motivated Jesus was the greatest motivation of all—pure, perfect, infinite love.

While serving in Chile during my first mission, I met a wonderful brother, Edward Howard. He was serving as a regional representative. We became friends, and following my mission we stayed in touch for years. I was deeply moved by this letter I received from him: "I have been spending most of my time now caring for Sister Howard. Since her stroke nearly three years ago she is like a rag doll. She can barely see. I am her 24-hour-a-day nurse. Because I love her it has been no great sacrifice. I often think love is what made the Lord's sacrifice somehow bearable for Him."

The Savior's motivation—so clear to us as members of His Church—is often doubted or misunderstood by many in the world. One man even tried to convince me I was wrong to thank Jesus for salvation. "Judas is the one you should be thanking," he said. "He is the one to praise and honor. Pilate and the Roman soldiers are the ones to thank, for if Judas had not betrayed Christ and Pilate had not ordered the soldiers to kill him, Jesus would never have done what He did."

How confused can people get? Jesus did not die because of Judas, but *for* Judas. Pilate tried to wash his hands of the blood of Christ, but Pilate's only hope for cleanliness is *through* the blood of Christ. The Roman soldiers were not taking Christ's life. He had "life in himself" (John 5:26) and chose to *give* it freely for them and for us.

FAITH AND WORKS

Just as we can see how confused that man was, many outside the Church believe that Mormons are equally confused. They believe we look beyond Jesus for our salvation. They see the efforts of Latter-day Saints to live the gospel and endure to the end as vain attempts to make up for our sins and save ourselves. Rather than seeing our works flowing from faith, they see the tasks we perform and callings we magnify as evidences that we believe we don't need a Savior. They see each dollar donated as a statement that we trust more in works than in faith. Perhaps they misjudge us because they are unable to see our motives. We certainly march to the beat of a drummer they don't hear—but it's not just a different drummer. It is *the* Drummer. Until they hear His music as we do, they won't understand why we move our feet.

"And may God grant, in His great fulness, that men might

be brought unto repentance and good works, that they might be restored unto grace for grace" (Helaman 12:24). We forgive others as Christ forgives us. We love others as He loves us. We serve others as He serves us—not in an effort to deserve grace, but to accept it and offer it to others as freely as it is offered to us.

Latter-day Saints teach early-morning seminary, make sack lunches for the homeless, avoid inappropriate entertainment, break bad habits, and sacrifice to travel to the temple not in place of faith, but as an inevitable outgrowth of our faith—not to *earn* grace, but to *return* grace for grace. Like Paul, we can say, "I may rejoice in the day of Christ, that I have not run in vain, neither laboured in vain" (Philippians 2:16).

The supposed conflict between faith and works seems as old as the scriptures themselves. Perhaps a resolution is difficult because debaters usually examine faith and works only on one level. Resolution can be found only when we consider what is *behind* the faith and *beneath* the works. Both faith and works are possible only through the Atonement, but both become a continuous part of our lives when we realize the continuous nature of the Atonement. This perspective allows us to consider the motives that enable us to find and maintain the essential balance between the two. The important question isn't, "Am I saved by faith or works?" Rather, it is, "What motivates each of them in my life?"

The poet Henry Wadsworth Longfellow (1807–1882) wrote the following lines:

The heights by great men reached and kept
Were not attained by sudden flight,

But they, while their companions slept,
Were toiling upward in the night.

I am far from being a poet, but I have taken the liberty of partnering with Longfellow and adding a few words to his:

If heights by great men reached and kept
Were not attained by sudden flight,
If they, while their companions slept,
Were toiling upward in the night,
Then what did motivate their climb?
What did companions never feel?
Was it fear or prize sublime?
Did obligation feed their zeal?
Each height by great men reached above
Is motivated out of love.

Chapter 10

A LESSON IN MARBLE

Repenting and remaking broken covenants allows us to feel a deep sense of gratitude to the Lord. In those moments of struggle, our needs are accentuated. When we experience our own Gethsemanes, we truly begin to value Christ's. When we recognize our own weakness, we stand in awe of His strength.

I had the opportunity of attending a wonderful youth conference in Olympia, Washington, along with singer/songwriter Kenneth Cope. The theme was "The Time Is Now." Dedicated leaders had gone to a great deal of trouble to decorate accordingly. There were clocks on the tables, clock faces on the walls, a big cardboard clock tower in the cultural hall, and a huge, glass-covered clock that sat on an easel toward the front of the chapel.

At the end of the conference, the young people gathered in the chapel for a testimony meeting. Everything was going as planned until, without warning, the easel broke and the clock came crashing to the floor. The noise of shattering glass startled everyone.

The young man who was in the middle of bearing his testimony at that exact moment handled it beautifully. "Well, I guess the time is no longer now," he said. "I guess the time is past!" Everyone laughed, as a few young people and leaders hurried to straighten the mess so the meeting could continue. This same young man finished his testimony by saying, "I'm sorry the clock broke. I guess it can no longer remind us of the theme, but it can remind us that God loves broken things."

He was alluding to a song Kenneth wrote and had performed at the conference—a beautiful song that assures us that even when we waste the time God has given and we end up feeling like that clock, God still loves us and can help pick up the pieces and move us forward.

Joseph Smith taught that *all* are within reach of pardoning mercy who have not committed the unpardonable sin (see *Teachings*, 191). President Boyd K. Packer confirmed, "Save for the exception of the very few who defect to perdition, there is no habit, no addiction, no rebellion, no transgression, no apostasy, no crime exempted from the promise of complete forgiveness. That is the promise of the Atonement of Christ" ("Brilliant Morning of Forgiveness," 7).

God doesn't condone sin, but He knows that broken covenants can lead to broken hearts, which can lead us to Him, the mender of all broken things. This process allows us to grow and gain charity as well as forgiveness and acceptance.

BROKEN COVENANTS CAN LEAD TO CHRIST

"But if covenants are broken," some may ask, "wouldn't it have been better to never have made them in the first place?" No. It is only in making covenants that we find the power to keep them, and it is only in keeping them that we find the power to endure.

We are never so aware of our need for air as when we are drowning. Repenting and remaking broken covenants allows us to feel a deep sense of gratitude to the Lord. In those moments of struggle, our needs are accentuated. When we experience our own Gethsemanes, we truly begin to value Christ's. When we recognize our own weakness, we stand in awe of His strength. Like starlight against a nighttime sky, when we see the darkness of our vices, we can also see the brightness of His virtues.

Sin is not the most ideal way to come to know Christ. No one should plan to sin just so he or she can feel close to the Savior any more than a married couple should plan to fight so they can make up. Such manipulated moments draw participants apart rather than closer. But even without our planning them, there are already enough sinful moments in our lives to make us painfully aware of how much we need Christ and His Atonement.

Not long after his baptism, my young son asked, "Dad, why do people cry when they talk about Jesus?" This boy had made covenants at the age of eight, but in his innocence he had not yet encountered the sins, transgressions, and struggles that would require Jesus' forgiveness and succoring. Until he felt that desperate need, he would continue to be baffled by the tears in the eyes of the rest of us.

Elder Richard G. Scott has said: "I know that every difficulty we face in life, even those that come from our own negligence or even transgression, can be turned by the Lord into growth experiences, a virtual ladder upward. I certainly do not recommend transgression as a path to growth. It is painful, difficult, and so totally unnecessary. It is far wiser and so much easier to move forward in righteousness. But through proper repentance, faith in the Lord Jesus Christ, and obedience to His commandments, even the disappointment that comes from transgression can be converted into a return to happiness" ("Finding Joy in Life," 26).

THE ATONEMENT LEADS TO LEARNING

"But wouldn't it be better," some may ask, "if we never sinned and never needed the Atonement in the first place?" The question itself is inaccurate, because even if all sin were completely avoidable (which it isn't), we would still need the Atonement. Little children never sin, but they still need the Atonement—not just to overcome the effects of the Fall but to give them the opportunity to learn and grow in their efforts to become Christlike.

The Book of Mormon teaches about how little children who die before reaching the age of accountability are saved through the grace of Christ (see Moroni 8). They do not need the tests in life and will need no test after this life (see Andrew C. Skinner, *Garden Tomb,* 138). The grace of Christ is seen not only in saving little children—who, as we are taught, go straight to the celestial kingdom—but in the doctrine taught by Joseph Smith that these spirits will be resurrected as children in the Millennium and raised to adulthood by their parents (see Smith, *Gospel Doctrine,* 453; McConkie, "Salvation of Little Children," 3). Children who die young need no testing and no forgiveness. Nevertheless, they will still benefit from the experiences, nurturing, and love they missed in this life. Although saved by Christ, they can still learn by experience.

Alma taught, "This probationary state became a state for

them to prepare; it became a preparatory state" (Alma 42:10). Although little children need no probation, they do need preparation, and that too is provided for through Christ's suffering.

The Savior suffered for every age, every dispensation, and every person. He took upon himself every sin imaginable as well as the multiple times offenses are repeated. "Hence the appropriate symbolism of His bleeding at each and every pore—not just some" (Maxwell, "Answer Me," 33).

No one can learn of the amount of suffering Christ endured without wishing it might have been reduced. I used to think we could do that by not sinning, but of course that is impossible. I also thought maybe we could have eliminated the need for Christ's suffering by never leaving the premortal existence. Now I understand that even a refusal to leave would not have spared God and Christ their suffering because it would have meant a complete rejection of the Father's plan for our eternal progress and Christ's central role in it. Such rebellion may have even brought God and Jesus *more* suffering than they were to endure through the process of the Atonement. Eliminating the Atonement would have meant we were automatically condemned by experience. Proceeding with it allows us to be taught by experience. Both were painful options, but one so much more than the other. The Atonement allows us to live and learn, but also to learn and live.

God and Jesus knew that life would be far from predictable and full of influences beyond our control. They knew we would inevitably sin and that sin would mean suffering for them and for us. But we all still chose that suffering over the alternative. After the Fall, Adam came to realize that because of the Atonement his experience with suffering and sin could lift him rather than pull him down. He exclaimed, "Blessed be the name of God, for because of my transgression my eyes are opened, and in this life I shall have joy, and again in the flesh I shall see God" (Moses 5:10). Eve too realized that through Christ and His gospel their sad experiences could actually exalt them. "Eve, his wife, heard all these things and was glad, saying: Were it not for our transgression we never should have had seed, and never should have known good and evil, and the joy of our redemption, and the eternal life which God giveth unto all the obedient" (Moses 5:11).

I remember as a young schoolteacher (with a large and active class) asking my wife, Debi, "When does life even out? Why does it always feel like a roller coaster with so many highs and lows all in the same day? I wish life would just level out."

Being a nurse, Debi replied, "Brad, when you get hooked up to the heart monitor, you don't want to see a straight line. That's bad news. It's the up and down lines that let you know you are alive."

The highs and lows let us know we are participating and not just observing, learning and not just existing. President Gordon B. Hinckley said, "I know it isn't easy. It's discouraging at times, sure. Aren't you glad it isn't just fun all the time? Those valleys of discouragement make more beautiful the peaks of achievement" (*Discourses*, 1:301).

LEARNING LEADS TO CHARITY

Sin, mistakes, sorrows, and injustices do not automatically make people more empathetic. Consider how the wars in the Book of Mormon softened and humbled the hearts of some, but hardened others (see Alma 62:41). It is Christ who can sanctify our experiences for our growth and development, but we must let Him do so. As our relationship with Him is strengthened, not only are we strengthened but we are also blessed with an increase of His love and charity.

Working on my Ph.D. at the University of Wyoming, I was required to take an advanced statistics course. I had completed the beginning courses several years earlier, but could remember very little. I had no idea how I was going to manage the requirements of an advanced class.

Several weeks into the semester, I was floundering. I approached the chair of my committee, Louise Jackson, and said, "This is really over my head. Usually I at least know enough about a subject to follow along. This time I am totally lost."

"Good!" she said. "You don't know how happy that news makes me."

Her response took me totally by surprise. Teachers are not usually glad when you announce that you are failing.

Dr. Jackson continued: "Remember how this feels. Memorize this moment. Don't ever forget this lesson. This is how many of your future students will feel, and you must be able to relate to them in order to understand and be effective in helping them." She then gave me some suggestions, including the names of a few possible tutors. She also arranged to meet with me regularly to review my progress—things she assured me she would never have done had she not also once struggled through a few difficult classes of her own.

FORGIVING AND REMEMBERING

We are often told we should forgive and forget. That's good advice when dealing with the sins of others, but when it comes to our own sins, I think we must forgive and *remember*. Once we have repented, we will no longer feel the sting of guilt and remorse associated with sin (see Alma 24:10), but we must not forget what we have learned from the experience. Through His atoning sacrifice, Christ takes away the pain and the stain, but not the memory. To remove the memory would eliminate the learning.

In the scriptures we see many examples of those who learned from their missteps. Mark, the author of the second Gospel, had earlier left his mission and deserted Paul and Barnabas (see Acts 12:25; 13:13; 15:37–38). The people of Melchizedek who went to join the city of Enoch (see JST, Genesis 14:34) had earlier "waxed strong in iniquity and abomination; yea, they had all gone astray; they were full of all manner of wickedness" (Alma 13:17). But "they did repent" (v. 18). Corianton, who was listed among the faithful who brought peace to the Nephites (see Alma 49:30), had earlier been chastened for being immoral on his mission (see Alma

39:3–5, 11). Look through the list of missionaries who served with Alma when he set out to preach among the sinful and apostate Zoramites (see Alma 31:5–7). The majority of them had all passed through a time of sin or apostasy themselves, yet they repented. Their imperfection gave them a reason to seek Christ, and now they wanted to help others do the same. In each case, God did not see their mistakes and sins as hopeless disasters. He saw them as growing pains.

Theoretically, a person could be declared free from the demands of divine justice by living his or her life perfectly, never taking a backward step, and never deviating one inch from the strait and narrow path. It could be said that the theoretical person was justified by law (see Millet, *Grace Works*, 69). I have heard some exclaim, "Wouldn't it be a glorious thing to be in such a state?"

I would have to say it wouldn't. Not only is such a life impossible, it would not even be desirable or lead to ultimate happiness. This theoretically justified person would still need to be sanctified, and sanctification requires a real relationship with God, the Savior, and the Holy Spirit. The Atonement is not just for the prodigal sons out there, but also for all their brothers and sisters who stayed home. It's not just for the thieves crucified next to Christ, but for the faithful disciples who looked on as well. No one can make it to heaven alone. We must have a covenant relationship with God and Christ, who can take the very ropes of sin that previously bound us down and lift us up. Remember that those who are forgiven of many sins have much love, and "to whom little is forgiven, the same loveth little" (Luke 7:47).

A LESSON IN MARBLE

"President, may I speak with you?" The words on the phone were soft and full of emotion. I quickly set an appointment for an interview. The elder who had called was strong, confident, and effective. He had surfaced as a leader among his peers long before he had been officially called to lead. He was a happy missionary who had learned to work hard and had experienced success in reaching the hearts of investigators and members alike.

The time of our interview arrived, and the young man and his companion were welcomed into the mission home. I invited his companion to wait for us in the other room while I sought a private place with my troubled missionary. "Elder, what's bothering you?" I began.

"I made a big mistake," he replied.

Inside I panicked. Noting the many mission rules and how easily they could be broken if the missionaries were not careful, my mind began to expect the worst. In that instant I imagined every possible problem that could have affected this elder's upcoming honorable release. "What was your mistake?" I asked hesitantly.

"I read *The Miracle of Forgiveness*," confessed the elder.

I laughed. "Reading the words of President Kimball is far from being a mistake."

"But now I realize that there are things I did when I was

younger that I should have confessed and never did. There were times when things went a little farther than what I actually told my bishop."

I listened quietly as he spoke. Nothing I was hearing was so grievous that it would have affected his worthiness to enter the temple or serve his mission. Still, those past sins were affecting him and his feelings of worthiness now. They needed to be confessed.

He said, "When I was younger I guess I just thought that these sins weren't all that big a deal, but the closer I get to the Lord, the worse I feel about them."

I explained that what he was experiencing was a very normal and natural step in his spiritual maturity—one through which we all pass. His repentance and full confession were healthy indicators that he was indeed drawing closer to God and the Savior.

"But President, I look back and see so many flaws. I remember all I have done and feel so ashamed and hypocritical. I know Jesus takes the sins away, but it is the memory of them that bothers me."

Remembering an analogy I had heard years earlier from Randy Boothe, director of the Young Ambassadors at BYU, I went to a nearby shelf and retrieved a marble egg that had been set there for decoration. I said, "Look at the marble. Isn't it beautiful?"

The elder nodded in agreement.

"What makes it beautiful is not that it is free from imperfections. If it were clear and white, with no flaws, it would look plastic and artificial. The marble is beautiful and useful *because* of the dark veins, not *in spite* of them. When we repent, our sins are gone, but the memories linger, just like these dark lines. However, as we keep our covenants and experience the sanctifying influence of the Spirit, it is as if those dark lines are polished over time. They actually become part of our beauty."

Nephi was not beautiful and useful to God just because he would "go and do the things which the Lord hath commanded" (1 Nephi 3:7), but because he could remember being a "wretched man" easily beset with "temptations and . . . sins" (2 Nephi 4:17–18). Alma was not beautiful and useful to Christ just because of his diligence in preaching repentance unto others (see Alma 4:19–20; 8:15–16; 13:21, 27), but because he could remember needing repentance himself (see Mosiah 27:2–19; Alma 36:11–17).

I testified to this young missionary, "One day when you stand before Christ, you too will be beautiful—just like the marble—not because you have no dark, jagged memories in your mind, but literally because you do, and because through repentance and confession you are willing to let Christ and the Holy Ghost sanctify and polish them."

We prayed together, and the young elder left the mission home feeling much better about having read President Kimball's book—and about himself. He finished his mission on a high note and with an enthusiasm I'll always remember.

Many missionaries leave Santiago airport with souvenirs. Some take typical Chilean clothing, ceramics, or wood carvings. Others take goodies to share with their families. They all have lots of pictures and letters from the people they have come to love. This elder was no different when his time came to go home. He was loaded down just like all the rest who were leaving. His arms were full of packages and carry-on bags. There was hardly room for one more souvenir, but I had a small gift I wanted to give him. When his turn came for one last *abrazo*, I slipped into his hand a small marble egg.

He looked at it, then at me. He said nothing. Neither did I. We both just smiled. One more *abrazo*, and he was off. As I watched him go—as I watched them all go—they looked wonderful to me. Their missions had not been easy. They all had passed through struggles and challenges, but they had learned so much and loved so freely. They had gone through their ups and downs and had their share of flaws and dark lines, but they were leaving stronger, wiser, and better for the experience. I knew the next few years would be difficult. They might slip up, but I knew the continuous Atonement of Jesus Christ would be there for them. The same Atonement that had gotten them to this point would continue to bless their lives as they journeyed forward. In that moment, I was able to see these valiant and noble missionaries just as their Savior did, and they glowed. To me they were as beautiful and valuable as polished marble.

SOURCES CITED

Backman, Milton V. *Joseph Smith's First Vision*. Salt Lake City: Bookcraft, 1980.

Ballard, M. Russell. *Counseling with Our Councils*. Salt Lake City: Deseret Book, 1997.

———. *When Thou Art Converted*. Salt Lake City: Deseret Book, 2001.

Bednar, David A. "Becoming a Missionary." *Ensign*, November 2005.

Benson, Ezra Taft. "The Book of Mormon and the Doctrine and Covenants." *Ensign*, May 1987.

Black, Susan Easton. *Finding Christ through the Book of Mormon*. Salt Lake City: Deseret Book, 1987.

Bytheway, John. *SOS: A Teenage Guide to Getting Home in Safety*. Salt Lake City: Bookcraft, 2000.

Callister, Tad R. "How Can I Lead a More Saintly Life?" In *Arise and Shine Forth: Talks from the 2000 Women's Conference*. Salt Lake City: Deseret Book, 2001.

Christofferson, D. Todd. "Born Again." *Ensign*, May 2008.

Cope, Kenneth. "Tell Me." In *All About You*. Salt Lake City: Shadow Mountain Records, 2008.

Covey, Stephen R. *The Divine Center*. Salt Lake City: Bookcraft, 1982.

Dew, Sheri. *God Wants a Powerful People*. Salt Lake City: Deseret Book, 2007.

———. "Our Only Chance." *Ensign*, May 1999.

Eyring, Henry B. "A Child of God." In *Speeches*. Provo, UT: Brigham Young University, 1998.

Faust, James E. "Unwanted Messages." *Ensign*, November 1986.

Givens, Terryl L. *By the Hand of Mormon: The American Scripture That Launched a New World Religion*. Oxford: Oxford University Press, 2002.

Hafen, Bruce C. "The Atonement: All for All." *Ensign*, May 2004.

———. *The Believing Heart*. Salt Lake City: Deseret Book, 1986.

———. *The Broken Heart*. Salt Lake City: Deseret Book, 1989.

———. *A Disciple's Life: The Biography of Neal A. Maxwell*. Salt Lake City: Deseret Book, 2002.

Hafen, Bruce C., and Marie K. Hafen. *The Belonging Heart*. Salt Lake City: Deseret Book, 1994.

Hafen, Marie K. "Eve Heard All These Things and Was Glad." In *Women in the Covenant of Grace: Talks Selected from the*

1993 Women's Conference. Salt Lake City: Deseret Book, 1994.

Hinckley, Bryant S., comp. *Sermons and Missionary Services of Melvin Joseph Ballard*. Salt Lake City: Deseret Book, 1949.

Hinckley, Gordon B. *Discourses of President Gordon B. Hinckley, Volume 1: 1995–1999*. Salt Lake City: Deseret Book, 2005.

Holland, Jeffrey R. "The Atonement of Jesus Christ." *Ensign*, March 2008.

———. *Trusting Jesus*. Salt Lake City: Deseret Book, 2003.

Holland, Patricia T. "God's Covenant of Peace." In *The Arms of His Love: Talks from the 1999 Women's Conference*. Salt Lake City: Deseret Book, 2000.

Hymns of The Church of Jesus Christ of Latter-day Saints. Salt Lake City: The Church of Jesus Christ of Latter-day Saints, 1985.

Journal of Discourses. 26 vols. London: Latter-day Saints' Book Depot, 1854–1886.

Kimball, Spencer W. *The Miracle of Forgiveness*. Salt Lake City: Bookcraft, 1969.

Lee, Janet. "Pieces of Peace." In *Every Good Thing: Talks from the 1997 BYU Women's Conference*. Salt Lake City: Deseret Book, 1998.

Lewis, C. S. *Mere Christianity*. San Francisco: HarperCollins, 2001.

Longfellow, Henry Wadsworth. "The Ladder of St. Augustine." In *Best-Loved Poems of the LDS People*. Edited by Jay A. Parry, Linda Ririe Gundry, Jack M. Lyon, and Devan Jensen. Salt Lake City: Deseret Book, 1996.

Lund, Gerald N. "Are We Expected to Achieve Perfection in This Life?" In *A Sure Foundation: Answers to Difficult Gospel Questions*. Salt Lake City: Deseret Book, 1988.

MacArthur, John F., Jr. *Faith Works: The Gospel According to the Apostles*. Dallas: Word Publishing, 1993.

Madsen, Truman G. "Man Against Darkness." In *Expressions of Faith: Testimonies of Latter-day Saint Scholars*. Edited by Susan Easton Black. Salt Lake City and Provo, UT: Deseret Book and Foundation for Ancient Research and Mormon Studies, 1996.

———. "The Suffering Servant." In *The Redeemer: Reflections on the Life and Teachings of Jesus Christ*. Salt Lake City: Deseret Book, 2000.

Mangum, Donald P., and Brenton G. Yorgason. *Amazing Grace: The Tender Mercies of the Lord*. Salt Lake City: Deseret Book, 1996.

Matthews, Robert J. *A Bible! A Bible!* Salt Lake City: Bookcraft, 1990.

Maxwell, Neal A. "Answer Me." *Ensign*, November 1988.

———. *Notwithstanding My Weakness*. Salt Lake City: Bookcraft, 1988.

———. "Swallowed Up in the Will of the Father." *Ensign*, November 1995.

———. *We Will Prove Them Herewith*. Salt Lake City: Deseret Book, 1982.

McConkie, Bruce R. *A New Witness for the Articles of Faith*. Salt Lake City: Deseret Book, 1985.

———. "The Salvation of Little Children." *Ensign*, April 1977.

McConkie, Joseph Fielding, Robert L. Millet, and Brent L. Top. *Doctrinal Commentary on the Book of Mormon, Volume 4*. Salt Lake City: Bookcraft, 1992.

Millet, Robert L. *Grace Works*. Salt Lake City: Deseret Book, 2003.

Nibley, Hugh. "Not to Worry." In *Expressions of Faith: Testimonies of Latter-day Saint Scholars*. Edited by Susan Easton Black. Salt Lake City and Provo, UT: Deseret Book and Foundation for Ancient Research and Mormon Studies, 1996.

Oaks, Dallin H. "The Challenge to Become." *Ensign*, November 2000.

———. *The Lord's Way*. Salt Lake City: Deseret Book, 1991.

———. *Pure in Heart*. Salt Lake City: Bookcraft, 1988.

———. *With Full Purpose of Heart*. Salt Lake City: Deseret Book, 2002.

Okazaki, Chieko N. "Lighten Up!" In *Women and Christ—Living the Abundant Life: Talks Selected from the 1992 Women's Conference*. Salt Lake City: Deseret Book, 1993.

Packer, Boyd K. "Atonement, Agency, Accountability." *Ensign*, May 1988.

———. "The Brilliant Morning of Forgiveness." *The New Era*, April 2005.

———. *Let Not Your Heart Be Troubled*. Salt Lake City: Bookcraft, 1991.

———. "Little Children." *Ensign*, November 1986.

———. *That All May Be Edified*. Salt Lake City: Bookcraft, 1982.

———. "'The Touch of the Master's Hand.'" *Ensign*, May 2001.

Pearson, Glenn L. *Know Your Religion*. Salt Lake City: Bookcraft, 1961.

Perry, Steven Kapp, "I Take His Name." In *Another Testament*. Provo, UT: Prime Recordings, 2001.

Preach My Gospel. Salt Lake City: The Church of Jesus Christ of Latter-day Saints, 2005.

Roberts, B. H. *The Gospel and Man's Relationship to Deity*. Salt Lake City: Deseret Book, 1966.

Robinson, Stephen E. *Believing Christ: The Parable of the Bicycle and Other Good News*. Salt Lake City: Deseret Book, 1992.

Scott, Richard G. "Finding Joy in Life." *Ensign*, May 1996.

Skinner, Andrew C. *The Garden Tomb*. Salt Lake City: Deseret Book, 2005.

Smith, Joseph. *History of The Church of Jesus Christ of Latter-day Saints*. 7 vols. Salt Lake City: Deseret Book, 1948–50.

———. *Lectures on Faith*. Salt Lake City: Deseret Book, 1985.

———. *Teachings of the Prophet Joseph Smith*. Selected and arranged by Joseph Fielding Smith. Salt Lake City: Deseret Book, 1976.

Smith, Joseph F. *Gospel Doctrine*. Salt Lake City: Deseret Book, 1939.

Smith, Lucy Mack. *History of Joseph Smith by His Mother*. Salt Lake City: Bookcraft, 1958.

Talmage, James E. *Jesus the Christ*. Salt Lake City: Deseret Book, 1983.

Twain, Mark. *The Adventures of Huckleberry Finn*. New York: Dodd, Mead & Co., 1953.

———. *Pudd'nhead Wilson*. New York: Pocket Books, 2004.

Uchtdorf, Dieter F. "The Infinite Power of Hope." *Ensign*, November 2008.

"We Believe." *Ensign*, March 2008.

Welch, John W. "The Good Samaritan: Forgotten Symbols." *Ensign*, February 2007.

Wells, Robert E. Unpublished family history shared with author. Used by permission.

Wilcox, S. Michael. *Fire in the Bones: William Tyndale—Martyr, Father of the English Bible*. Salt Lake City: Deseret Book, 2004.

INDEX